In an age when church leaders are bombarded with programs, approaches, techniques and initiatives, it can be overwhelming to know what is the essential work of a pastor. My friend Kyle Bueermann has clearly and succinctly identified from a biblical standpoint to what a pastor should devote himself. This book needs to be in every pastor's library and is a great resource experienced pastors could share with younger pastors.

Mark Clifton, *Senior Director for Church Replanting North American Mission Board*

In *They Devoted Themselves,* Bueermann succinctly walks through Acts 2:42-47 with an eye towards church health and revitalization. His insights would assist any pastor in the work of establishing a biblical model to ensure a healthy church that can lead to the revitalization of local congregations. I would encourage pastors to read this work.

Kenneth Priest, *Director Convention Strategies, Southern Baptists of Texas Convention; Interim Director of the Center for Church Revitalization, Southwestern Baptist Theological Seminary*

Bueermann and I share a mutual heartbeat of calling the 21st century church back to the practices of the first century church in Acts. In his book, Bueermann has done this by focusing on the summary passage of the Jerusalem church (Acts 2:42-47). Bueermann has effectively put the spotlight on this beautiful God-given sketch of a healthy church.

Bob Burton, *Multiplication Pipeline Consultant, North American Mission Board*

This was an encouragement and resource that, as a pastor of a replanted church, I greatly needed. Dr. Bueermann interactively guides readers through core beliefs of the first century church while grappling with issues ' This book helps us get back to f what the church today should b

Dusty Marshall, *Past* exico

In a time when many congregations are asking questions about their future, *They Devoted Themselves* focuses on the right conversation for pastors and their lay leaders in order to ensure a hopeful future. With practical applications and tools for any pastor in the midst of a church revitilization, this book can help today's congregations recalibrate based on biblical principles and reverse their drift toward irrelevance in their community.

James Nugent, *Church Revitalization Director, South Carolina Baptist Convention*

THEY DEVOTED THEMSELVES

THEY
DEVOTED
THEMSELVES

what churches in the 21st century can learn
from the Church in the 1st century

KYLE BUEERMANN

ACOMA PRESS

Requests for information should be addressed to:

Acoma Press
40 W. Littleton Blvd. Suite 210, PMB 215
Littleton, CO 80120

www.acomapress.org
info@acomapress.org

Cover Design & Interior Layout: Evan Skelton

First Printing, 2020

Printed in the United States of America

Paperback ISBN: 978-1-7354826-2-0
PDF ISBN: 978-1-7354826-3-7

To Michelle, Noah & Hailey.
I'm blessed to walk through this life with you.

CONTENTS

FOREWORD

While I wish I did not have to learn the lesson the hard way, one of the first lessons I learned as a pastor was you could not merely preach a church healthy. Please do not get me wrong: preaching is vitally important, and pastors should faithfully engage the text of Scripture week in and week out. God uses our faithful preaching (and even our flubs here and there) to grow the people He has called us to shepherd.

Early on in my ministry, however, I thought preaching was *it*. I thought if I could have the evangelistic effectiveness of Billy Graham, the awesome alliteration of Adrian Rogers, the passionate proclamation of John Piper and the expert exposition of Alistair Begg, I would have the "Midas touch" on any church I served. Of course, I am not Graham, or Rogers, or Piper, or Begg, I am Matt Henslee. While I am an evangelistic, alliterating, passionate expositor, I soon learned ministry was about far more than delivering faithful sermons.

In Acts 2:42-47, the Lord has given us a potent recipe for healthy church life that, at times, has been ignored in many modern churches ... including mine. I had a devotion to Scripture on lock, but I was not as apt to be devoted to fellowship, prayer, worship and evangelism. Do not get me wrong -- I loved me some potlucks, I prayed, I sang and I evangelized, but it took a few years to learn ministry that honors Christ is more than a weekly sermon, quarterly potluck, sparsely attended prayer meetings and so forth.

To lead a church that honors Christ, I needed a glimpse of the early church's devotion to a few things that have been lost or obscured over the years. In fact, more than a glimpse, I now know that I need a full grasp on the how and why of this Acts 2 early church "recipe." I needed to gain a realization that the five characteristics of a church named there are effective for ministry 365 days a year and will be the only way I can lead a church that truly honors Christ and lasts long after I am gone.

I encourage you to grab your Bible, a highlighter, a pen and a journal, and dig deep into the book you are about to begin, because it is more than a book, it is a blueprint for a ministry that glorifies God as His Word prescribes.

Matt Henslee
Pastor of Mayhill Baptist Church
Mayhill, New Mexico

PREFACE

The book you hold in your hands is the culmination of a dream I have had. It focuses on a passage of Scripture that has haunted me in the most beautiful way for almost 15 years. It is a passage that still keeps me awake at night.

My first introduction to Acts 2:42-47 was when I was a youth pastor at First Baptist Church of Kermit, Texas. I was leading our students through a study by Doug Fields called "Church as It Should Be." That study led students through the book of Acts over six weeks. In the session that focused on Acts 2:42-47, something stopped me in my tracks. I was struck by the description of how the early church went about their business in the days following Pentecost. I have never recovered.

Even now, when I read that passage, I am transported to the dusty streets of first century Jerusalem. I picture many things in that scene of the first church in action:

- I see Peter boldly proclaiming the gospel to a multitude gathered on the day of Pentecost. I see many men, women, and children - Luke later notes there are 3,000 - who place their faith in Christ Jesus.

- I imagine the line stretching for blocks as those first believers wait for their baptism as followers of Jesus.

- I picture the joy -- the laughter, tears, and maybe even fear on each face -- as they move from death to life and to a wonderful new life they can't even fully grasp yet.

- I am in awe that many of those baptized will lose their lives because they refuse to renounce the Savior who gave His life for them. I walk with those first believers to the daily times of prayer in the temple, I take in the fragrances of baking bread and frying fish in the homes where believers will gather to hear a sermon from Peter, James, or John.

- I feel the weight of personal sacrifices as poor believers sell their possessions and bring the money to the apostles to meet the needs of their brothers and sisters in Christ. I feel the sense of community they felt.

Lest I over-spiritualize these early believers, let's remember these were men and women with doubts, fears, and sins they battled against. These were people with jobs and families, who lived in communities with real life issues just like those we face today. And yet, these people lived with faith in something – or, rather, Someone – who changed everything for them. They lived with the hope, joy, and purpose that only followers of Jesus can possess.

The life of those first century believers described in Acts 2:42-47 is an example to 21st century believers today. As I look at how the early believers went about their daily lives as followers of Christ, I am going to draw your attention to how we are – and how we are not – following their example. We do not have the luxury of going back and conducting detailed surveys of how many believers in the early church spent time memorizing the words of Jesus or what percentage of their day was spent in prayer. However, what we have in Scripture is sufficient to give us a good picture of how the early believers went about their daily lives (2 Tim. 3:16-17). I also include many statistics from different studies over the past decade and a half to ask whether or not our lives look like those of the early believers in Acts.

Along the way, we are going to face some harsh realities about large gaps in our discipleship. My goal in presenting these gaps is not to beat us up. Rather, my prayer as we look at statistics that are less than encouraging is that we will be spurred on to recover a biblical view of discipleship and church health.

I am writing this amid a COVID-19 pandemic that has hit our nation – and the world – very hard. At the moment, almost every single one of the pastors and churches I know has ceased to meet in-person for the past two months as part of the much larger effort in our culture to slow the spread of the virus. There are many questions about what things in our culture, and even in the church, will look like once we return to "normal life" – whatever "normal" turns out to be.

Even in all the uncertainty, however, I am sure of this: God's church will not be stopped. And I think that maybe, just maybe, the answer to how we will do church when we can gather in person again is not to invent something new, but to look back to something ancient. And I think that maybe, just maybe, the answer is found in Acts 2:42-47.

I invite you to come on this journey with me. Let's leave a world of Netflix and Fortnite behind and go to a world of sandals and crosses. In doing so, let's discover what it looks like to be a part of a church that devoted themselves deeply to one another and, more importantly, to the Savior.

chapter 1

THEY DEVOTED THEMSELVES...
TO CHRIST

If anyone wants to follow after me, let him deny himself, take up his cross, and follow me.
Matthew 16:24

When Christ calls a man, he bids him come and die.
Dietrich Bonhoeffer[1]

The 1969 New York Mets are a great example of what happens when a group of people is devoted to a single task. Before '69, the Mets were the epitome of lousy baseball. In their inaugural season in 1962, they finished with a record of 40-120, which turned out to be the most losses by a team in a single season in the 20th Century. Things did not improve quickly after that first season. In fact, in their first seven seasons (1962-1968), the Mets never finished higher than ninth in a ten-team division. Before 1969, they had only one season – 1966 – when they had a record above .500 after the third game of the year. That is a rough eight seasons of baseball!

The 1969 season did not start off any better. Through the first 41 games, the team amassed a record of 18-23. After that, however, they went on an 11-game winning streak that began to turn their season, and franchise, around. On August 13, the Mets were still 10 games behind the first place Chicago Cubs, which is usually considered an almost insurmountable deficit with less than two months left in the season. The Mets needed a miracle.

The Mets proceeded to win 14 of their last 17 games in August. In September and October, they went 24-8 to finish the season with a division-winning record of 100-62, eight games ahead of the second place Cubs. The "Amazin' Mets," so nicknamed by their former manager Casey Stengel, went on to defeat the Baltimore Orioles in five games to win the World Series, becoming the first expansion team in Major League Baseball history to win the Series.

The Amazin' Mets of 1969 achieved unprecedented success because they devoted themselves to playing winning baseball. They did not let the previous seven seasons of atrocious baseball define them and in 1969, they made history.

Devoting Ourselves

The 1969 Mets are an example of what happens when a group of people devotes themselves to something. In Acts 2:42, we are told that the members of the first church devoted themselves to something as well. In that passage, Luke writes, "They devoted themselves to the apostles' teaching, to the fellowship, to the breaking of bread, and to prayer."

For a long time, I missed the full scope of what the believers devoted themselves to. I would read this passage and see the first part of the first sentence: "they devoted themselves to the apostles' teaching" and I would stop there. I would think, "okay, for us (since we no longer have apostles), this would be the Bible (more on this in the next chapter). So, I should be devoted to the Bible. Got it."

There is no question that Christ followers *should* be devoted to Scripture. I believe it is vitally essential for believers to study Scripture. I also think there is a reason that the apostles' teaching is listed *first* in Luke's list in Acts 2. However, it is not the only thing in that list, and to single out one item to the exclusion of all the others would be to do ourselves – and those we teach/lead/mentor – a great disservice. As the Lord has graciously worked in my life over the years, I have come to realize that there is a foundational truth underlying the "devotion list" of the early church in Acts 2:42-47. The church in the first century was devoted to this list because they were first devoted to Christ. All of these activities the first believers were devoted to – the apostles' teaching, breaking of bread, prayers, meeting together in homes and in the temple – were a means to an end of their devotion to Christ Jesus. Let's take a look at what Jesus said about the nature of devotion to Him.

Devotion to Christ

The Greek word for "devoted to," *proskartero,* used in Acts 2:42-47 appears only 10 other times in Scripture. A brief look at two of these instances will reveal its' definition. In Mark 3:9, Jesus uses the word to tell the disciples to have a boat ready for Him, lest the crowds crush Him. In that verse, the word expresses the need to be ready to go at a moment's notice. In Romans 13:6, Paul uses the word when he talks about paying taxes to authorities who *attend to* upholding justice. These two instances teach us that there is both a sense of urgency and responsibility conveyed in the word. We see both of these demonstrated in how the early believers followed Christ.

In Luke 14, Jesus delivers a challenging message about what it means to be devoted to Him. In verse 25, Luke tells us that great crowds are accompanying Jesus. They are following Him to listen to Him, but I think maybe even more than that, they followed Him to see Him perform some amazing miracles. At this point in Luke's gospel, the crowds have watched Jesus feed the 5,000, cast out demons, heal a woman stricken with a disease for the past 12 years, and bring a 12-year-old girl back to life. The crowds have seen some pretty impressive stuff. Jesus developed quite a following of fans. But Jesus isn't interested in making crowds of people happy. He's interested in calling people to be fully devoted disciples.

So, He turns to the crowd and tells them some of the hardest words in all of the New Testament: "If anyone comes to me and does not hate his own father and mother, wife and children, brothers and sisters—yes, and even his own life—he cannot be my disciple" (Luke 14:26). Jesus is saying that there is an urgency to following Him and that it carries great responsibility.

Is Jesus really saying that I have to hate my mom, my dad, my wife, my kids, and my brother, or else I can't really be his disciple? Well, yeah. But not in the way you may think. He's not saying that you should walk up to your mom and say, "Mom, I have decided to follow Jesus. So, from now on, you are my enemy. No more talking or texting. You're dead to me." God's Word will never contradict itself, and we are clearly told in the Ten Commandments that we are to honor our parents. When Jesus says in Luke 14 that we must hate father and mother, He is using hyperbole to make a point.

What He is saying, by using hyperbole, is that we must not love anyone, or anything, more than we love Him. We must not be devoted to anyone or anything more than we are devoted to Him. On the surface this may sound obvious but, in practice, it is much more difficult.

John Calvin called the human mind "a perpetual forge of idols."[2] We can so easily become devoted to so many things that take our attention off of Christ; things like money, success or health. Jesus reminds us, however, that even good things become idols if we are *devoted* to them above Him.

To help us understand, we can consider Jesus' calling of the first disciples. In Luke 5, Jesus goes for a walk by the Sea of Galilee. As he's walking along the beach, he comes across two brothers – Simon Peter and Andrew. Verse 19 says Jesus called out to them, "Follow me, and I will make you fishers of men." Now, these two guys were faced with a significant life decision. Their fishing business was their livelihood. It probably defined not only what they did, but even who they were: they were fishermen. Jesus' call to them confronted them with a question: would they continue to be devoted to their business, or would they leave everything and follow Him? Matthew tells us that they immediately dropped their nets and followed Jesus. They responded with devotion, with a sense of urgency.

Jesus strolls a little farther down the beach with his new disciples and sees two other guys who were also fishermen, James and John. These guys are not only fishermen, they are working in their father, Zebedee's, fishing *business*. Again, Jesus issues the call to follow Him. James and John, too, are faced with a life-changing decision. Social customs would dictate that they should remain with their father and help him with his business. I mean, after all, they just got back from fishing, and there's a lot of work to do. Wouldn't it be acceptable to meet up with Jesus later? They had a lot of responsibility to think about in helping run the family business.

However, Matthew tells us that, like Andrew and Peter, these men immediately left their boat and their nets to follow Jesus. It is also important to note that they left not just their boat and their nets, but their father.

I certainly do not think James and John hated their father. In fact, I think they probably loved him and felt a great deal of devotion to him! After all, fishing was not easy work. It required long hours with stinky fish. And yet, when Jesus called, they immediately left everything. They loved their father a lot, but they chose to love Jesus above even him. Following Jesus carried the greatest sense of urgency and the highest level of responsibility. That is Jesus' point in Luke 14: to be His followers we must love Him and be devoted to Him more than anything else, above everyone else.

Different Responses to Jesus

Wouldn't it be great if everybody responded to Jesus like these four men did? Wouldn't it be awesome if everyone who heard the gospel immediately left their old ways and their old lives and followed Him? Well, it would be incredible, but that is not reality. In fact, I am willing to go out on a limb and say it won't even happen *most* of the time. In Luke 9:57-62, Luke gives us three different pictures of people who reject the opportunity to follow Jesus.

The first man in this story approaches Jesus and says, "I will follow you wherever you go." This is entirely unsolicited. He wants to be a follower of Jesus. However, Jesus responds to him, "Foxes have holes, and birds of the air have nests, but the Son of Man has nowhere to lay his head." Now, the gospel writers never tell us how this man responds to Jesus. But, since we are not told that he immediately followed after Jesus as the disciples did, we can assume he walks away. He was more devoted to his comfort than following Jesus.

Jesus calls out to the second man, "Follow me." This man responds with what at first seems like a reasonable request, "Let me first go and bury my father." Jesus' response is, "Leave the dead to bury their own dead. But as for you, go and proclaim the kingdom of God." Now, at first, this seems really harsh, doesn't it? You mean to tell me this guy can't even go and bury his father?

The problem here is that we are not told that this man's father has died yet. It could be that his father is beginning to age, and this son feels the responsibility to stick around until his father is dead. Was this a bad desire? Not necessarily. It is possible that he was a caring and obedient son. It is also at least plausible that his father was wealthy, and he wants to wait for his father to die so he can receive his inheritance. However, whatever the case, something was more important than his devotion to Jesus. And that kept him from obeying the call of God upon his life.

The final man in this passage also approaches Jesus. He says, "I will follow you, Lord, but let me first say farewell to those at my home." A lot of people are like this guy. "Lord, I want to follow you, but first let me graduate." "When I get married, then we'll get involved in a church." "When we start making more money, then we'll start giving faithfully." "I'll start serving in that ministry after our kids are out of the house." "Pastor, we've just been so busy. We'll be back when things settle down." See, the truth is that we give our immediate attention to the things most important to us. Jesus called this man to immediate devotion. He was more devoted to those at home. Jesus responds, "No one who puts his hand to the plow and looks back is fit for the kingdom of God." This may seem unreasonable, but he was exposing the true affections of this man's heart.

The call to follow Jesus is a call to immediate obedience and full-fledged devotion. So, how do you respond when God calls you? Are you like the disciples who immediately leave everything and follow after Him, or are you like these last three who looked for reasons *not* to follow Him?

We are not often given a clear picture of how the New Testament authors viewed their own writings. One exception to this is found in 2 Peter 1:20-21, where Peter seems to understand that he is writing something similar to the Old Testament Scriptures. Did the other New Testament authors realize they were writing Scripture as well? We saw above that the writers clearly understood they were conveying essential details about the life, ministry, death and resurrection of Christ. They believed that their writings could lead someone to faith in Christ and help provide assurance of eternal life. But does that mean that they considered their own writings to be on the same level as Scripture? Not necessarily. But wait, we are not quite done yet.

Perhaps a more important question than whether the New Testament authors considered their writings to be Scripture or not is this: did the readers of the apostles' writings consider them to be Scripture? A telling example of how the early church viewed the teaching of the apostles comes in 2 Peter 3:15-16. Here, Peter writes,

> Also, regard the patience of our Lord as salvation, just as our dear brother Paul has written to you according to the wisdom given to him. He speaks about these things in all his letters. There are some matters that are hard to understand. The untaught and unstable will twist them to their own destruction, as they also do with the rest of the Scriptures.

Peter refers to Paul's writings alongside "the rest of the Scriptures." So, by the time Peter wrote his second letter, he considered Paul's letters to be on par with Scripture. This is interesting because it shows that, while at least some of the apostles were still alive, their writings were considered to have the same authority as the Old Testament Scriptures.

Thus, we can see that the teachings of the apostles were considered Scripture by first century believers. By the mid-60s AD, the apostles began to write down their teachings for others to read. By the end of the first century, all of the apostles' writings that we now know as the New Testament were completed. Local churches began compiling lists of the writings that they considered authoritative, and, over many years, lists of commonly accepted writings were circulated. Eventually, the 27 books that we now have as the New Testament were finally agreed upon by the councils of Hippo (AD 393) and Carthage (AD 397).[4]

The Greek word that Luke uses in Acts 2:42 to refer to the apostles' teaching is the word *didache*. That word carries the weight of both instruction and doctrine. It could also be said that the early church devoted themselves to the apostles' doctrine. The early believers sought to believe the same things about Jesus that the apostles believed. And the New Testament is the recording for all time of what the apostles taught.

John Stott helpfully summarizes,

> Since the teaching of the apostles has come down to us in its definitive form in the New Testament, contemporary devotion to the apostles' teaching will mean submission to the authority of the New Testament.[5]

Scripture in American Churches

The official doctrinal statement of the Southern Baptist Convention, *the Baptist Faith & Message 2000*, says this about Scripture,

> The Holy Bible was written by men divinely inspired and is God's revelation of Himself to man. It is a perfect treasure of

divine instruction. It has God for its author, salvation for its end, and truth, without any mixture of error, for its matter. Therefore, all Scripture is totally true and trustworthy. It reveals the principles by which God judges us, and therefore is, and will remain to the end of the world, the true center of Christian union, and the supreme standard by which all human conduct, creeds, and religious opinions should be tried. All Scripture is a testimony to Christ, who is Himself the focus of divine revelation.[6]

Another statement that was drafted to explain what modern Evangelicals believe about the Bible is the Chicago Statement on Biblical Inerrancy. That document, adopted in 1978, says,

Holy Scripture, being God's own Word, written by men prepared and superintended by His Spirit, is of infallible divine authority in all matters upon which it touches: it is to be believed, as God's instruction, in all that it affirms; obeyed, as God's command, in all that it requires; embraced, as God's pledge, in all that it promises.[7]

I think you will be hard-pressed to find any two statements that explain an understanding of Scripture in clearer language than these two paragraphs. These two statements affirm that evangelical followers of Christ believe the Holy Bible is the infallible, inerrant and inspired Word of God.

While official statements about what we believe are important, it is also important to ask do modern followers of Christ *actually* believe what these statements affirm? As church leaders and disciple-makers, we need to ask what Americans in general, and Christians in particular, believe about Scripture. Do believers in the United States in the 21st Century hold the same convictions about Scripture that the early believers in Acts did? Are we as devoted to Scripture as they were?

Over the past two decades, there have been numerous studies conducted on the spiritual lives of Americans as a whole, as well as those who claim to be followers of Christ. In his work, *The Shape of Faith to Come*, Brad Waggoner discovered that only 54% of churchgoers strongly agreed with the statement, "The Bible is the written word of God and is totally accurate in all that it teaches."[8] Another 18% said they agreed somewhat with the statement. Waggoner is quick to point out that, when someone becomes a follower of Christ, they may not automatically develop a deep knowledge of spiritual truths. Obviously, biblical knowledge does not happen through osmosis. A deep understanding of the truths of Scripture requires time devoted to reading and studying Scripture.

How are Americans doing in that department? Waggoner discovered that only 16% of churchgoers said they read the Bible every day, with another 20% saying they read it a few times a week.[9] So, just over one-third of those who said they attended church regularly indicated that they read the Bible at least a few times a week. Perhaps the biggest irony in this is that we have more access to Scripture today than perhaps any other generation in history. We have a multitude of translations available in a multitude of formats in print, digital and audio mediums. And yet, at the same time, we may be the most biblically illiterate generation in history as well.

In 2017, Pew Research discovered, "About a third of Americans (35 percent) say they read Scripture at least once a week, while 45 percent seldom or never read scripture."[10] It is important to note that this study was not limited to just churchgoing Evangelical Christians. Pew's research covered followers from many religious groups regarding how often they read whatever their religion considers Scripture. Among religious groups, Jehovah's Witnesses (88%) and Mormons (77%) represented the highest number of those who said they read Scripture weekly. This study found that 66% of Evangelical Protestants said they read Scripture daily.

While that number is more encouraging than Waggoner's, the Pew study also discovered some concerning facts about what Christians really believe about Scripture. "While about four-in-ten Christians (39%) say the Bible's text is the word of God and should be taken literally, 36% say it should not be interpreted literally or express another or no opinion. A separate 18% of Christians view the Bible as a book written by men, not God."[11]

Let that sink in for a moment. Only about 40 percent of those who claim to be followers of Christ say they consider the Bible to be the Word of God! Obviously, this stands in stark contrast to what the early followers of Christ in Acts believed and what the Bible says about itself.

Recovering a Devotion to Scripture

In his book, *Spiritual Disciplines for the Christian Life,* Donald Whitney says, "No Spiritual Discipline is more important than the intake of God's Word. Nothing can substitute for it. There is simply no healthy Christian life apart from a diet of the milk and meat of Scripture."[12] Whitney continues, "Regardless of how busy we become with all things Christian, we must remember that the most transforming practice available to us is the disciplined intake of Scripture."[13] Despite Whitney's words, from the research noted above, we see that devotion to Scripture is severely lacking in many believers' lives today. How can the

21st century church recover the devotion to Scripture that characterized the early church? How can we return to the fundamental devotion to the apostles' teaching that Acts 2:42 talks about?

It Begins in the Pulpit.

First and foremost, pastors have the responsibility to faithfully proclaim the Word of God. I do not have the space to address a full theory of preaching here (though I will look more at preaching in chapter 5 when I discuss worship), but I will briefly defend the practice of expositional, text-driven preaching. That is, a practice of preaching through books of the Bible and allowing the central theme of the text to become the main theme of the sermon.[14] If the people we are called to shepherd as pastors are going to grow in their understanding of the Bible as the Word of God, it requires preachers who are demonstrating week in and week out how Scripture speaks to our daily lives.

I have seen first-hand how preaching straight through books of the Bible has consistently led me to preach particularly timely passages, even when I planned out my preaching calendar months in advance. For instance, when the COVID-19 crisis hit the United States in widespread fashion in March 2020, I was preaching through Mark's gospel. I planned out my preaching calendar for the entire year in December 2019. At that time, it was unthinkable that we would face a pandemic of such magnitude that would effectively shut down life as we know it for many weeks.

On March 15, 2020, the final Sunday our church was able to meet in person for a couple of months, I preached Mark 1:29-

34, a passage about Jesus healing Simon Peter's mother-in-law from a fever. The passage also tells about Jesus healing many others who were sick and casting out demons from many who were afflicted. I had this passage on the calendar a couple of months ahead of the pandemic. Yet, on that particular Sunday, I was preaching to our people about the power of Christ over diseases and demons. That provided the perfect opportunity to call our congregation to continue trusting Christ in the middle of the biggest health crisis our nation had experienced in 112 years.

I am certainly not smart enough to plan things with such precision, but God is! And His timeless, unchanging, inerrant and infallible Word speaks powerfully in any circumstance we may face. This is just one example of many I have experienced during my ministry that has convinced me of the power of God's Word to speak if we will only allow it to speak. You do not have to dress up God's Word with fancy props or catchy taglines. Simply proclaim it boldly and see what happens!

It Continues at Home.

As Whitney noted above, there is no substitute for devotion to Scripture in spiritual formation. While a commitment to expository preaching on the part of the pastor is essential, that alone will not create a congregation that is devoted to Scripture. In addition to sitting under expositional preaching, men and women must *daily* immerse themselves in God's Word. Thankfully, as I mentioned above, we have unprecedented access to God's Word. The Bible is available in thousands of languages and across multiple platforms in print and digital formats through the technology of the internet. The YouVersion Bible app has hundreds of reading plans to take you and your people through sections - or even the entirety - of Scripture. You can encourage your people to read through plans on their own or create a group on the app and read through portions of Scripture together.

As I write this, I am leading a group from our church in reading through the New Testament in 30 days on the Bible app. For those who are not technologically savvy, we emailed out a PDF to our church members so they could print out a hard copy of the reading plan. Some in your congregation may be like my wife who is technologically savvy, but prefers a hard copy of a reading plan over using an app.

Daily time reading and meditating on God's Word is crucial to the spiritual health of individual believers and our churches as whole. Acts 2 tells us that the first century church devoted themselves to the apostles' teaching and we would be wise to follow suit.

Prayer for the Journey

Father, Your Word declares that it is living and active, and is profitable for teaching, reproof, correction and training in righteousness (2 Tim. 3:16-17). Help us to be people who believe that it can do just that. We repent of our complacency toward Your Word. Help us to proclaim it with boldness and help those of us who fill Your churches to immerse ourselves in Your Word. Amen.

TAKE ACTION

— · — · — · — · — · —

1. Read 2 Timothy 3:16-17. How is Scripture profitable for teaching? For reproof? For correction? For training in righteousness? Give specific examples where possible.

2. How are you challenged by the early believers' devotion to Scripture? How does your own experience match up to theirs?

3. What are some things you can do, beginning today, to increase your devotion to God's Word?

Further reading on Scripture:

- *Living by the Book* by Howard & William Hendricks
- *Spiritual Disciplines for the Christian Life* by Donald S. Whitney

chapter 3

THEY DEVOTED THEMSELVES...
TO FELLOWSHIP

Now all the believers were together and had all things in common. They sold their possessions and property and distributed the proceeds to all, as any had need.
Acts 2:44-45

Any organ that is detached from the body will not only miss what it was created to be, it will also shrivel and die quickly. The same is true for Christians that are uncommitted to any specific congregation.
Rick Warren[15]

At the beginning of my freshman year of college, the university I attended, Wayland Baptist University in Plainview, Texas, held a new-student orientation weekend for incoming freshmen and transfer students. It was a time to meet other incoming freshmen, learn the layout of the campus and familiarize ourselves with college life. The whole weekend had the feel of a summer church camp. We were divided into small groups. We participated in some small group Bible studies, a scavenger hunt and messy games -- like a royal rumble style wrestling match on a giant tarp covered in dry dog food that had been thoroughly soaked until it became roughly the consistency of quicksand. Good times.

Do you know what they called this weekend? They called it *Koinonia*. That was my first introduction to that word. As an 18-year-old incoming religion major, I didn't yet know anything about the Greek language. I remember some kind of passing comment during that weekend that *koinonia* was the Greek word for fellowship. But that didn't really click with me. Mostly, when I heard the word *koinonia* for the next couple of years, I remembered the smell of rotten wet dog food as I tried unsuccessfully to salvage the clothes I wore during that game.

A couple of years later, in my elementary Greek class, I came to understand that the idea behind the Greek word *koinonia* goes quite a bit deeper than scavenger hunts and messy games. It goes beyond potlucks and meet and greet times during a worship service. *Koinonia* describes a deep bond of fellowship that can only exist between persons who realize the bond they have as those who have been redeemed by Jesus from the power of sin and death.

Fellowship in the Early Church

Acts 2:42 tells us the early church devoted themselves to the fellowship and the breaking of bread. What does Luke mean when he says they devoted themselves to the fellowship, to the *koinonia*? Bill Mounce explains that *koinonia*, "can refer to the mutual interests and sharing of members in the community of faith, the church ... Such sharing involved not only associating with each other, but also sharing food and other necessities of life."[16]

The idea behind the word *koinonia* is a deep sharing of life. It goes beyond a surface-level relationship to suffering, crying, rejoicing, laughing, serving, giving, ministering and worshipping together. In the New Testament, this fellowship, this deep level of relationship, led the early believers to share meals, possessions, their homes and their very lives with each other.

In Acts 2, Luke focuses on two primary ways *koinonia* took place. The local church fellowshipped through the sharing of meals and the sharing of possessions.

Shared Meals

Throughout Luke's gospel, we continuously see Jesus sharing meals with others. In fact, I think you would be hard-pressed to find an example of Jesus eating alone at any point in that gospel. The early believers apparently followed this example because Luke writes that they were devoted to the "breaking of bread." I. Howard Marshall, in his commentary on Acts, says this term probably refers both to eating regular meals together and observing the Lord's Supper.[17]

Paul goes on to describe how the church in Corinth practiced the Lord's Supper. In 1 Corinthians 11:17-34, it seems possible that a larger meal was observed than the little cup of juice and square cracker that have marked the observance of communion in Christianity's recent history. So, it is likely that the early church observed the Lord's Supper in conjunction with a larger fellowship meal. And they observed it regularly. The early church often shared meals together.

Shared Possessions

Luke describes how the early church shared possessions in two places. The first is in Acts 2:44-45. Here he writes, "Now all the believers were together and had all things in common. They sold their possessions and property and distributed the proceeds to all, as any had need." The bond the early believers felt toward one another led them to actually sell their stuff to meet needs within the church body. To provide a modern-day illustration, if "Bart" lost his job and needed some money for groceries, "Dave" and his wife would hold a garage sale to raise some money to help meet that need. If the Marshall family had some unexpected medical bills that put them deep in debt, the Watts family would take some money out of their savings account to help pay off the bills.

As I said above, this is far different from how we tend to view the idea of fellowship today. In fact, in the first century, this was a pretty radical idea, too. Kent Hughes writes, "This kind of fellowship did not exist before the giving of the Holy Spirit at Pentecost. The Greek word used here (*koinonia*) is not even found in the Gospels."[18] In other words, the word *koinonia* describes a uniquely-Christian practice that emerged in the life of the early church. It is a practice that developed out of the Holy Spirit's mighty move on the day of Pentecost earlier in Acts 2.

The second place Luke talks about the sharing of possessions is in Acts 4:32-37. He writes,

Now the entire group of those who believed were of one heart and mind, and no one claimed that any of his possessions was his own, but instead they held everything in common. With great power the apostles were giving testimony to the resurrection of the Lord Jesus, and great grace was on all of them. For there was not a needy person among them because all those who owned lands or houses sold them, brought the proceeds of what was sold, and laid them at the apostles' feet. This was then distributed to each person as any had need. Joseph, a Levite from Cyprus by birth, the one the apostles called Barnabas (which is translated Son of Encouragement), sold a field he owned, brought the money, and laid it at the apostles' feet.

There was not a needy person among the church body because of the generosity of the believers: what a testimony! Keep in mind this was before the days of social security benefits and Medicare. There were no unemployment benefits from the Roman government. Instead, the church took care of those within their fellowship who had financial hardships. I wonder if, in our own culture, we have come to rely too much on the government and not enough on the local church body to meet needs in the lives of those in our churches and communities.

It is important to note the difference between the early church's voluntary sharing of possessions with the forced communism of the mid-20th Century. Nowhere in the biblical record do we have any indication of a forced sharing. Rather, John Stott explains,

> Although in fact and in law they continued to own their goods, yet in heart and mind they cultivated an attitude so radical that they thought of their possessions as being available to help their needy sisters and brothers.[19]

It seems clear that those within local churches maintained private ownership of their own property. In the case of Barnabas in Acts 4, he sold a piece of property he owned, then brought that money to the apostles to be used to meet needs. While the sharing of goods was voluntary, caring for needs within the community of faith was nonetheless considered an essential part of the life of fellowship in the early church. This life of fellowship did not happen without obstacles. Real, authentic fellowship is a fragile thing. In Acts 5, Luke recorded Ananias and Sapphira's story, who were struck dead for lying about the amount of money they received when they sold a piece of property they owned. It is possible that Ananias and Sapphira recognized the praise given to Joseph for his act of generosity and believed they could fabricate the same results. Hughes explains:

> Ananias and Sapphira had witnessed Barnabas' magnificent act and had seen the great respect that it drew from fellow believers. So they announced they too would sell their property and give it to the church. However, they both agreed to claim to give the entire sale amount but hold some back, making everyone think they had given it all. If this happened today, Ananias would probably wait until the organ was playing 'I Surrender All' and then haltingly come forward, laying his check at Peter's feet. Ananias and Sapphira's ruse was not a mere miscalculation in their checkbook but premeditated deception. This was pious pretense — religious sham — simulated holiness — Christian fraud.[20]

The big problem behind Ananias and Sapphira's deception was not just the amount of money they gave - or did not give. The big issue was they were seeking the glory that belonged to the Lord alone. And the Lord will not share His glory with another.[21]

Turning our attention back to the early church's fellowship, Mark Dever argues that sharing possessions and goods is a key part of the meaning of church membership. "If you just hang out by yourself and refuse to join a church, other Christians can't help you. You're sailing your own little ship your own little way."[22] On the other hand, he continues, "The New Testament shows clearly that our following Jesus is supposed to involve care and concern for each other . . . And although we do it imperfectly, we should be committed to doing it."[23]

For the early church, the shared life of fellowship characterized the early church. The sharing of meals and possessions were two expressions of the deep fellowship that existed.

Fellowship in American Churches

In a study published in January 2019, Lifeway Research discovered that two-thirds of American young adults who attended church regularly for at least a year as a teenager said they dropped out for at least a year between the ages of 18 and 22.[24] The study discovered several reasons for this dropout rate:

> The five most frequently chosen specific reasons for dropping out were: moving to college and no longer attending (34 percent); church members seeming judgmental or hypocritical (32 percent); no longer feeling connected to people in their church (29 percent); disagreeing with the church's stance on political or social issues (25 percent); and work responsibilities (24 percent).[25]

While it was not listed as the number one reason, it is still significant that almost one-third of young adults who dropped out of church attendance said they no longer felt connected to the people in their church. In his study on the state of the American church, Waggoner found that only 27% of church attendees strongly agreed they had developed significant relationships in their church.[26] Both of these studies reveal a disturbing trend: fewer Americans are attending religious services. A significant contributing factor in this trend is a lack of fellowship among believers.

In *Being the Body,* Chuck Colson and Ellen Vaughan state, "Surveys show that the number-one thing people look for in a church today is fellowship."[27] While this may indeed be true, keep in mind that Waggoner discovered that only 27% of believers "strongly agreed" that they have developed significant relationships in their church. Another 33% said they "agreed somewhat."[28] It is disturbing when less than one-third of people surveyed can confidently say they have deep relationships inside their church family.

This reality echoes what Andy Stanley and Bill Willits write in their book *Creating Community:* "Although we drive on overcrowded freeways to catch overbooked flights and sit in jam-packed airplanes, we live in isolation."[29] They continue, "In the midst of our crowded existence, many of us are living lonely lives."[30] In a world where we are, theoretically, more "connected" than ever through the technology of the internet and social media, it seems that people are still longing for deep personal connections.

Pastor Harry Reeder writes that, in his many years of pastoral ministry, he has observed that, "New members must develop at least three new meaningful relationships within the first six months of their involvement in the body life of the church."[31] Reeder says this is one of the key pieces of assimilating or, as he puts it, "enfolding"[32] new believers and members into a local church. "If your church is to go from embers to a flame . . . you need to create community in the church."[33]

During the writing of this book, people in many countries across the world engaged in a period of social distancing and quarantine due to the COVID-19 crisis. The vast majority of churches in affected areas ceased meeting in-person for a time as part of the larger cultural effort to slow the spread of this disease. During that time, believers ached to gather in the same room to worship God. As a pastor, I can tell you that preaching to a video camera in an empty sanctuary is a poor substitute for being able to shake hands and hug the necks of the folks in our church body. I believe Colson and Vaughn are correct that the number one desire for people in seeking a church home is fellowship. God designed human beings with a desire for fellowship.

How Can We Recover a Devotion to Fellowship?

German theologian Dietrich Bonhoeffer wrote, "The Christian cannot simply take for granted the privilege of living among other Christians."[34] He continued, "It is by God's grace that a congregation is permitted to gather visibly around God's word and sacraments in this world."[35] These statements serve as a reminder to believers that fellowship, while important, is not a given for any believer. The development of deep community takes work.

In 1 Corinthians, Paul explains in detail the importance of community in the local church. In 1 Corinthians 12, he describes a local church as the body of Christ. "Now you are the body of Christ, and individual members of it" (1 Cor. 12:27). Warren, commenting on this verse, says, "*Any* organ that is detached from the body will not only miss what it was created to be, it will also shrivel and die quickly. The same is true for Christians that are uncommitted to any specific congregation."[36] (Emphasis his.)

There is a popular saying, "There are no lone ranger Christians. Even the Lone Ranger had Tonto." God designed Christians to grow as they live in community with other believers.

If we neglect this vital aspect of the Christian life, we do so to our own peril.

In his outstanding book on Christian discipleship, *Conformed to His Image*, Kenneth Boa writes, "Conversion to Christ and to the cross should lead in turn to conversion to community. Kingdom living is about loving and serving God and others."[37]

When I think of a church that really fellowships well, I think of Mayhill Baptist Church in the small mountain community of Mayhill, New Mexico, where my friend Matt Henslee serves as pastor. I am not sure I have seen a church filled with people that enjoy being around one another more than Mayhill. I have had the privilege of being at several services that were followed by potluck meals, and the joy in that room is infectious. Mayhill is a community of around 50 people and Mayhill Baptist regularly has 150 people in worship on Sunday mornings. Not only that, but many of the people drive 20-30 minutes to get to the church on Sundays.

Why would they do that? Is it because the preaching is phenomenal? Matt is a great preacher, but I am quite certain he would be the first to tell you that has very little to do with why people are willing to make an hour-long round trip on Sundays. People come from all over the area to attend church in Mayhill because there is a tangible feeling of deep fellowship within the body of Christ gathered there. Additionally, I have seen several occasions where very real, very pressing needs arose within the church body at Mayhill, and the members gave generously above and beyond their regular tithes and offerings to meet those needs. Every time I spend time with people in that church, I leave excited about increasingly getting to experience something like it among the church body that I serve.

There is something special that happens when believers come together to fellowship as the body of Christ. Fellowship obviously goes much deeper than merely being happy to be around one another and play games together. We saw in Acts 2 and 4 how the believers shared their possessions and belongings to meet needs within the church. We saw that people did not view their possessions as their own, but instead shared them with the church for their brothers and sisters who needed them more. I pray we can learn from the early church's example and devote ourselves to fellowship. (And it is even better if that fellowship includes fried chicken and banana pudding!)

Prayer for the Journey

Father, it seems we are living in an increasingly individualistic culture. We have more devices to stay connected with one another, yet we may be more disconnected than ever. Help us to not live our lives in isolation from one another, but instead lean into community with one another. Help us to realize that we need other believers in our lives, and they need us in their lives. May we come to know something of the deep fellowship that existed in the early church in Acts. Amen.

TAKE ACTION

— · — · — · — · —

1. Think back over the past six months of your church calendar. Can you point to specific things that have helped promote fellowship in your church? What were they and how did they enhance the fellowship?

2. Are there any that have detracted from or hindered the church's fellowship? What caused them to have such a negative impact?

3. Read Acts 4:32-37. Are there any needy persons in your congregation? If so, what are some tangible things your church could do to help meet those needs?

Further reading on fellowship:

- *Life Together* and *Prayerbook of the Bible* by Dietrich Bonhoeffer
- *Creating Community* by Andy Stanley and Bill Willits

chapter 4

THEY DEVOTED THEMSELVES...
TO PRAYER

Pray constantly.
1 Thessalonians 5:17

If I say that during the fifty-four years and nine months that I have been a believer in the Lord Jesus Christ I have had thirty thousand answers to prayer, either in the same hour or the same day that the requests were made, I should not go a particle too far. Often, before leaving my bedroom in the morning, have I had prayers answered that were offered that morning, and in the course of the day I have had five or six more answers to prayer, so that at least thirty thousand prayers have been answered for the self-same hour or the self-same day that they were offered.
George Müller[38]

I can think of no better human example in recent history of a man of prayer than George Müller.[39] Müller modeled a life of dependence upon God in prayer. Müller established orphanages that housed thousands of children during his lifetime that came with great financial cost, yet he made a vow that he would not ask any man for a monetary donation. He wholeheartedly believed the promise of Scripture in Philippians 4:19: "And my God will supply all your needs according to his riches in glory in Christ Jesus."

In his autobiography, Müller recounts numerous times when the orphanages were down to their last bit of money with no bread or milk for the children. After praying, Müller's family often received a knock at the door from an individual bringing just enough bread, or milk, or money to provide for that day's needs. Although Müller passed away nearly a century and a half ago, his life serves as a shining example of one who, like the early church, devoted himself to prayer.

Acts 2:42 says that the early believers devoted themselves to prayer. What exactly does that mean? Kent Hughes writes, "The text most likely suggests specific prayers, probably both Jewish and Christian. The early believers suddenly saw the old formal prayers through new eyes and also, in their new joy, created new prayers for praise."[40] Let's look at how prayer played a significant role in the life of Christ, the corporate life of the early church as well as privately among its individuals.

Prayer in the Life of Christ

Throughout the gospels, we discover that prayer was a primary commitment of the Lord Jesus Christ. As the disciples spent time with Jesus, there is no doubt that they observed Him praying often. In the early days of Jesus' earthly ministry, Mark writes, "Very early in the morning, while it was still dark [Jesus] got up, went out, and made His way to a deserted place; and there He was praying" (Mark 1:35).

Peter and the other disciples apparently woke up, realized Jesus was gone and went hunting for him. "Simon and his companions searched for Him, and when they found Him they said, 'Everyone is looking for you'" (Mark 1:36-37). While we certainly do not have every instance of Jesus' prayer life recorded in the gospel accounts, we do see that prayer was a priority for the Savior.

Apparently, seeing Jesus praying so much made an impact on the lives of the disciples. In Luke 11:1, Luke notes, "[Jesus] was praying in a certain place, and when He finished, one of his disciples said to Him, 'Lord, teach us to pray, just as John also taught his disciples.'" Writing on this passage, Steve Gaines notes that the disciples did not ask Jesus "how to preach, how to grow a Sunday School, how to establish a seminary . . . how to build a sanctuary or how to collect financial offerings. They asked Jesus to teach them to pray."[41] Dietrich Bonhoeffer, commenting on the same passage, wrote, "So spoke the disciples to Jesus. In doing so, they were acknowledging that they were not able to pray on their own; they had to learn."[42]

In His response to the disciples' request asking them to teach them to pray, Jesus gives the disciples – and us – what we now know as the Lord's Prayer:

> He said to them, "Whenever you pray, say,
> 'Father, your name be honored as holy.
> Your kingdom come.
> Give us each day our daily bread.
> And forgive us our sins,
>   for we ourselves also forgive everyone in debt to us.
> And do not bring us into temptation'" (Luke 11:2-4).

In the gospel accounts, Jesus assumes that followers of Christ will pray. In several places, Jesus is quoted as saying, "And *when* you pray . . ." (Matthew 6:5, 6, 7, 9; Luke 11:9; 18:1. emphasis mine).

Luke writes, "He often withdrew to deserted places and prayed" (Luke 5:16). Even on the night Jesus was arrested, Luke recorded that Jesus was praying. He commanded His disciples, "Pray that you may not fall into temptation" (Luke 22:40). Luke recorded that Jesus walked about a stone's throw away and prayed. "When he got up from prayer and came to the disciples, he found them sleeping, exhausted from their grief" (Luke 22:45). Reflecting on the prayer life of Jesus, Gaines writes,

> "No one ever prayed like Jesus. When it comes to prayer, He truly is the 'expert.' While on earth, Jesus prayed with a depth of intimacy that is unmatched. He communed with God through thanksgiving, petition, intercessions, and spiritual warfare. No one ever prayed like the master.[43]

On the night before He was arrested, the apostle John wrote that Jesus "looked up to heaven" and prayed (John 17:1). As Jesus faced the most trying hour of his life, He went to the Father in prayer. Jesus modeled a life of prayer for His disciples and expected that they would follow His example.

Prayer in the Early Church

A call to prayer in Scripture is not confined to the gospel accounts. The books of Colossians and 1 Thessalonians contain commands to pray, "Devote yourselves to prayer" (Colossians 4:2), and "Pray constantly" (1 Thessalonians 5:17). In Acts 4:31, Luke declares that, after the believers prayed, "the place where they were assembled was shaken." James writes, "The prayer of a righteous person is very powerful in its effect" (James 5:16). The early church was devoted to prayer both corporately and individually.

Corporate Prayer in the Early Church

The book of Acts includes several instances of the church gathering together for prayer. For example, Luke records that the believers met every day "in the temple, and . . . from house to house" (Acts 2:46). This likely included both formal times of prayer and corporate worship, as well as times of informal, personal prayer and worship. John Stott notes that Luke's description speaks of the early church meeting for "prayer services or meetings (rather than private prayer)."[44] The early believers not only prayed when they gathered for formal meetings at the temple but they also prayed corporately when they spent time together during the week.

In Acts 3:1, Luke writes, "Peter and John were going up to the temple for the time of prayer at three in the afternoon." In the early days after Pentecost, followers of Christ continued meeting in the temple for the appointed hours of prayer.

In Acts 12, Luke talks about Peter's miraculous release from prison by an angel of the Lord. Acts 12:5 says the church "was praying fervently" for Peter. In Acts 12:12, Luke records that "many had assembled and were praying" for Peter at the house of John Mark's mother. In addition to the regular times of prayer at the Temple, Acts 12 shows believers gathering under special circumstances praying for Peter during his imprisonment.

Luke writes in Acts 13:3 that, as the church in Antioch was worshiping, the Holy Spirit spoke and told them to set apart Paul and Barnabas: "Then after they had fasted, prayed, and laid hands on them, they sent them off." The narrative in Acts demonstrates that corporate prayer was clearly a key part of the life of the early church.

Private Prayer in the Early Church

After Paul and Silas were arrested for casting a demon out of a slave girl, Acts 16:25 says, "About midnight, Paul and Silas were praying and singing hymns to God, and the prisoners were listening to them." While there were undoubtedly others present, this was a time of private prayer and worship in the lives of Paul and Silas.

The command to "pray constantly" In 1 Thessalonians 5:17 is a call to both corporate and private prayer. Clearly, the local church is not gathered continuously together, therefore this command applies to private prayer in the life of every individual believer.

In the early church, prayer took place corporately in places like the temple and from house to house and individual believers also engaged in prayer privately on their own. We would do well to follow this example of the early church in the life of the church today.,[45] So how are we doing?

Prayer in American Churches

In a 2001 study, researcher George Barna found that 97% of believers said they prayed to God in a typical week.[46] In a 2007 survey of churchgoers, Brad Waggoner found that 36% said they pray every day. Another 26% say they set aside time for prayer a few times a week, and 10% do so once a week."[47] Waggoner's numbers come to a total of 72% of people who said they pray at least once a week. So, in two studies just six years apart, the number of believers who said they prayed weekly dropped by 25%!

In 2015, Pew Research discovered that one-third of adults ages 18-29 said they seldom or never prayed, while 41% said they prayed at least weekly. Compare this to 55% of adults ages 50-64 and 36% of adults 65 and older who said they prayed at least weekly. Sixty-four percent of adults ages 30-49 said they prayed weekly, while 28% said they seldom or never prayed.[48] Combining the data for these different age brackets, this survey shows the majority of American adults (71%) claimed to pray at least weekly, while 55% claimed they prayed at least daily.

Taking these three studies, conducted over a period of 15 years, into account, a picture begins to emerge. While most individuals who claim to be followers of Christ said they pray at least once a week, about one-third of believers said they either never pray or did so irregularly.

How can we recover a devotion to prayer?

The evidence from the life of Christ and the lives of the early believers shows that prayer was meant to be an essential part of the Christian life. As mentioned above, the early believers described in Acts 2 met every day to worship and pray together. However, based on the research presented above, it appears 21st century believers in the United States do not put the same emphasis on prayer that existed in the early church.

As pastors and church leaders, if we want to see the prayer lives of our church members increase, we must first model that for them. Are you spending time in the Father's presence to deepen your own relationship with Him? Are you praying frequently for those you are responsible for leading? Are you pleading with Him on behalf of your lost friends and family members?

I will be the first to admit that this is an area in which I have struggled. But I am also glad to say it is an area in which the Lord is growing me immensely.

One tool the Lord has used in my life in this area is the book *Pray for the Flock* by Brian Croft and Ryan Fullerton. In this book, Croft and Fullerton remind pastors that, as shepherds of God's flock, we need to intercede to the Chief Shepherd on behalf of our people. In the appendix of the book, the authors offer perhaps the single most useful tool I have seen to foster consistent prayer for the people in your church.

The tool is a basic template for praying through your church membership roll. Croft and Fullerton suggest taking your church roll, and dividing the individual members (or families, depending on the size of your church) throughout the first 28 days of the month. This will lead you to pray for the people in your church by name every single month.

The membership of the church I serve, First Baptist Church of Alamogordo, New Mexico, has 57 family units as I write this. So, I took these families and divided them up over the course of the month. Using this method, I will pray for two or three families each day for 26 days. That leaves, in a typical

30-day month, four days where I do not have a specific family to pray for. On those days, I pray for 27) church planters and replanters, 28) missionaries, 29) fellow pastors and local churches, and 30) folks I know who do not know Christ.

I keep the guide in the front of my Bible, so it is always right at hand. In addition to serving as a prayer guide, this tool has enhanced my shepherding of the flock that God has entrusted to me as pastor. On the days I pray for a family, I have an opportunity to mail a card, send a text message or make a phone call to check in on them and let them know that I prayed for them. I can tell them it is a joy to serve as their pastor, and ask how our church can help them grow in their relationship with the Lord. And all that takes less than half an hour! I also shared the prayer guide with our deacons and some other key leaders in my church so that we now have several people praying through our membership each month.

When it comes to congregational prayer, Bob Burton's *The Spiritual DNA of the Early Church* is a fantastic resource. Burton surveys the book of Acts and identifies 10 characteristics that made the early church "turn the world upside down," as Luke describes it in Acts 17. Burton is quick to point out that none of what happened in the book of Acts happened without prayer.

Using the acrostic ACTS (Adoration; Confession; Thanksgiving; Supplication), Burton provides a 10-week prayer guide for leading your church in corporate prayer. While 10 weeks is a relatively short period, this prayer guide can serve as a catalyst to a revival of prayer in your church. I have included a link to the 10-week prayer guide in the section "Further Reading on Prayer" at the end of this chapter.

Brothers and sisters, we must be people of prayer! I will close this chapter with a phenomenal quote from Kenneth Boa:

> [Prayer] is the meeting place where we draw near to God to receive his grace, to release our burdens and fears, and to be honest with the Lord. Prayer should not be limited to structured times but should also become an ongoing dialogue with God as we practice his presence in the context of our daily activities.[49]

Prayer for the Journey

Father, I repent of all the times I have let other things get in the way of my spending time in prayer with you. Cultivate in me a heart that desires to spend time with you in prayer. Help me to model a life of prayer for those you have entrusted to me. Thank you for your grace that forgives me when I fall short. Amen.

TAKE ACTION

1. Do you have a systematic approach for praying through your church membership roll? If not, read back through the description of Brian Croft and Ryan Fullerton's simple prayer guide, then make your own based on your church's membership.

2. Of all the things that the disciples could have asked Jesus to teach them, why do you think they specifically asked that He teach them to pray?

3. Read through the "As you pray" passages from the gospels (Matthew 6:5, 6, 7, 9; Luke 11:9; 18:1). Then, take the next 15 minutes, get alone, and spend some time in prayer. Consider using the ACTS prayer acrostic from Bob Burton listed below.

Further reading on prayer:

- *Pray Like It Matters* by Steve Gaines
- *Spiritual Disciplines for the Christian Life* by Donald S. Whitney
- *Prayer: Finding the Heart's True Home* by Richard Foster
- *Pray for the Flock* by Brian Croft and Ryan Fullerton

Further reading on George Muller:

- *George Muller: Delighted in God* by Richard Steer-
- *The Autobiography of George Muller* by George Muller

Practical prayer resources:

- "ACTS Prayer Guide" by Bob Burton, available at http://bobburton.net/images/resources/Acts_Prayer_GuidesCh urch_Genome_Project.pdf

  This is a simple 10-week prayer guide that you can use in your church's corporate prayer gatherings or in your personal times of prayer. It will lead you to pray for your community using the ACTS model (Adoration, Confession, Thanksgiving, Supplication).

- *The Valley of Vision: A Collection of Puritan Prayers and Devotions* edited by Arthur Bennett
- *5 Things to Pray for Your City* by Pete Nicholas and Helen Thorne

chapter 5

THEY DEVOTED THEMSELVES...
TO WORSHIP

— · — · — · — · — · —

Therefore, brothers and sisters, in view of the mercies of God,
I urge you to present your bodies as a living sacrifice, holy and
pleasing to God; this is your true worship.
Romans 12:1

Worship — the way the Bible explains it to us — is not just seen
from the outside. It's more than just a set of observable
activities that, once completed, equals a worship experience
with the one true God.
Mike Harland [50]

Human beings are, at our core, worshipers. God has hardwired into us a desire to seek something or someone bigger than ourselves that we can adore and praise. But just because we have a God-given desire to worship does not mean that our worship is automatically directed towards the only Being truly worthy of our worship. In fact, in the fallen state of humanity, I think the exact opposite is true. We are bent toward worshiping things *other than* the Creator. John Calvin was spot on in his assessment that "the human mind is, so to speak, a perpetual forge of idols."[51]

We see this every week as millions of people gather in stadiums or in front of television sets to cheer on their favorite teams. There are dozens, possibly hundreds, of websites devoted to nothing more than the latest gossip about celebrities ranging from Tiger Woods to the Tiger King. A random selfie taken by a random actor before he even gets out of bed in the morning can garner millions of likes and thousands of retweets.

All of us – every single human – is guilty in some way of what Paul said in Romans 1:21: "Claiming to be wise, they became fools, and exchanged the glory of God for images resembling mortal man, birds, four-footed animals, and reptiles." While most of us have probably never literally bowed down to an idol, we have all allowed things to take the central place that only God should have in our lives.

In reality, our culture is really no different than much of the culture of the first century Roman empire. In that culture, idols and false worship were rampant. In fact, in Acts 19, Luke describes a riot that broke out against Paul. In that account, people were turning from their worthless idols to faith in Christ. A local silversmith who made literal idols of the false goddess Artemis realized his business was suddenly being impacted. In response, he created quite a disturbance against Paul and his companions. They were literally fighting against Paul to protect the idols of their false goddess. We might laugh at that scene a bit, but are we really any different when someone threatens the idols we hold close?

Worship of the One True God

Don Whitney explains that our English word "worship" comes from an old-English word *weorthscype*, which eventually morphed into *worthship*. He says, "To worship means to ascribe the proper worth to God, to magnify His worthiness of praise, or better, to approach and address God as He is worthy."[52]

In Acts 2, we see that the believers in the early church devoted themselves to worship. In verse 46, Luke tells us that the believers met together in the temple every day. We have already looked at how the early church seemed to genuinely enjoy being together, and how they shared a deep bond of fellowship with one another. Now we turn our attention to how they gathered together to worship.

Worship in the Early Church

Like the fellowship and prayer life of the early church, worship happened in both corporate and individual settings. John Stott says,

> They did not immediately abandon what might be called the institutional church . . . At the same time, they supplemented the temple services with more informal and spontaneous meetings (including the breaking of bread) in their homes.[53]

Certainly, the early believers understood that gathering regularly as a corporate body to worship the risen Savior should be a priority for every follower of Christ.

While the word "worship" never occurs in Acts 2:42-47, the concept of worship is undoubtedly present. *Proskyneo*, the Greek word most commonly translated as *worship* in the New Testament, means "to fall down and/or worship' someone or something."[54] Although it can also refer to pagan worship, it is most often used to refer to worship directed toward God the Father or Christ Jesus the Son. The word translated in Acts 2:47 as "praising," *ainountes*, is only used to refer to praise of God in the New Testament.[55] Acts 2:42-47 thus makes the point that the early believers were focused on worshiping God exclusively, and they did this both corporately and individually.

In corporate worship gatherings, we have seen how the church devoted themselves to partaking of the Lord's Supper and to prayer. In this section, I will focus on the corporate worship elements of music, preaching and financial giving.

Music in the Early Church

Worship leader Bob Kauflin asks, "Does God even care whether or not we use music to worship him? Apparently so. The Bible's longest book is a collection of songs."[56] This is a reference to the book of Psalms. Throughout the New Testament, believers worship God through singing. After Jesus instituted the Lord's Supper, Matthew 26:30 records Jesus and His disciples singing a hymn. In Ephesians 5:19, Paul commands the believers to speak "to one another in psalms, hymns, and spiritual songs, singing and making music with your hearts to the Lord."

The early believers in Acts had access to the Psalms, which they may have used as a hymnbook. In addition to the Psalms, Bill Mounce notes, "believers apparently sang newly written songs sung in honor of Christ."[57] The pattern of singing in the New Testament involved singing both older songs (the Psalms), as well as newer songs.

Preaching in the Early Church

In addition to music, preaching occupied a central part of the corporate worship gatherings in the early church. In 2 Timothy 4:1-2, Paul issued a strong charge to his young apprentice in the ministry, Timothy:

> I solemnly charge you before God and Christ Jesus, who is going to judge the living and the dead, and because of his appearing and his kingdom: Preach the word; be ready in season and out of season; rebuke, correct, and encourage with great patience and teaching.

Paul not only commanded Timothy to make preaching a priority, he modeled it for Timothy. In Acts 28:23, Luke explains, "From dawn to dusk he (Paul) expounded and testified about the kingdom of God. He tried to persuade them about Jesus from both the Law of Moses and the Prophets."

The priority of preaching was evident not only in the life of Paul but also in the lives of all of the apostles. Stephen Lawson writes, "The apostles' ministry of preaching and teaching is mentioned more often than any other activity in which they were engaged . . . No matter where they were, these apostles were preaching."[58] Paul and the other apostles made preaching a foundational part of their ministry.

Financial Giving in the Early Church

As we saw in Chapter 3 on fellowship, the early believers gave of their possessions and contributed financially to a local church. In that chapter, we examined the story of Joseph, also called Barnabas. He sold a piece of property he owned and laid the money at the apostles' feet. This is the first specific account in the book of Acts of members of the first church in Jerusalem contributing financially to the church.

In 2 Corinthians 8, Paul tells about believers in Macedonia who contributed generously to his ministry. In verses 1-5, he says,

> During a severe trial brought about by affliction, their abundant joy and their extreme poverty overflowed in a wealth of generosity on their part. I can testify that, according to their ability, and even beyond their ability, of their own accord, they begged us earnestly for the privilege of sharing in the ministry to the saints, and not just as we had hoped. Instead, they gave themselves first to the Lord and then to us by God's will.

In the next chapter, Paul told the Corinthian believers, "Each person should do as he has decided in his heart—not reluctantly or out of compulsion, since God loves a cheerful giver" (2 Corinthians 9:7).

Similarly, in 1 Corinthians 16:1-2, Paul instructed his readers, "Now about the collection for the saints: . . . On the first day of the week, each of you is to set something aside and save in keeping with how he is prospering." John MacArthur comments on this passage, "The point is that giving must occur regularly, not just when one feels generous, particularly led to do so, or instructed to do so for some special purpose."[59] Paul did not advocate for the taking of funds by force but, rather, called believers to give cheerfully.

Throughout the book of Acts corporate worship gatherings of the early church included the elements of music, preaching and financial contributions for the work of ministry.

Corporate Worship in
American Churches

In the previous section, we saw that Acts 2:42-47 explains that the first believers regularly met for corporate worship. Hebrews 10:24-25 commands believers to continue meeting together regularly. Given this biblical example and command, do American believers in the 21st Century see corporate worship as an integral part of their spiritual lives?

While it is no secret that worship service attendance has declined in the United States over the past few years, you may be shocked to see just how rapidly it has declined.

In 2008, Brad Waggoner discovered that 44% of those who claimed to be believers attended church services at least four times a month, and 18% attended five or more times per month.[60] He noted, "Attendance more than four times a month is possible if opportunities such as midweek services are counted."[61] So he discovered that 62% of believers attended some type of corporate gathering at least weekly.

That same year, Pew Research discovered that, across all faiths, 39% of adults in the United States attended religious services weekly. In comparison, 33% indicated they attended once a month or a few times each year.[62] By 2014, the number of weekly attendees had dropped to 36% while the number of those who attended monthly or a few times a year remained at 33%.[63]

Both of these studies show a decrease from George Barna's survey in 2001, which found that 63% of evangelical believers attended a worship service in a typical week.[64]

In October 2019, Pew Research released an article titled "In U.S., Decline of Christianity Continues at Rapid Pace."[65] That article states,

> Over the last decade, the share of Americans who say they attend religious services at least once or twice a month dropped by 7 percentage points, while the share who say they attend religious services less often (if at all) has risen by the same degree. In 2009, regular worship attendees (those who attend religious services at least once or twice a month) outnumbered those who attend services only occasionally or not at all by a 52%-to-47% margin. Today those figures are reversed; more Americans now say they attend religious services a few times a year or less (54%) than say they attend at least monthly (45%).[66]

These surveys show corporate worship attendance in the Unites States is declining steeply. This should cause those of us who are church leaders to lament. But it should also cause us to ask why this is the case.

In my personal experience in ministry, I can think of numerous examples where families would attend the Sunday morning worship gathering "unless something came up."

Maybe you have heard some of these all too familiar refrains:

- "We're going to the lake again this weekend."

- "The kids' soccer league has games every Sunday morning for the next two months."

- "We've just been so busy, and we needed to sleep in on Sunday morning."

While the weekly worship gathering is not the end-all, be-all of the Christian life, it is nonetheless a critical component. I do not know any church or pastor that expects all of their people to be in attendance for each of the 52 Sundays each year. However, if a large number of your members are only in corporate worship one or two Sundays each month, that shows a significant issue with their understanding of the importance of the weekly Sunday worship gathering in the life of the church. To better understand how this lack of prioritization has developed, let's look at the same three elements of music, preaching and financial giving in American churches today.

Music in American Churches

I grew up in the 1990s, at the height of what we now refer to as the "worship wars." As a teenager, I specifically remember one conversation where an older gentleman publicly asked a candidate for the worship pastor position at my home church, "You are not going to make us sing those ditties, are you?" I honestly still have no idea exactly what he meant, but he was sure adamant about it. Later, as a youth and music pastor in the mid-2000s, I experienced first-hand some of the backlash that occurred over singing newer praise songs versus traditional hymns.

Thankfully, for the most part, it seems that the worship wars have died down. While there are, no doubt, some churches that still wrestle with the balance of singing new versus old songs, we no longer hear about worship pastors regularly being fired because they dared bring in a guitar and drum set.

While the worship wars were a cultural phenomenon from the 1980s to the mid-2000s, they were not unique in church history. Bob Kauflin says, "Christians have been arguing about music in worship for centuries. And it hasn't always been pretty."[67] Kauflin continues by explaining in the 18th Century,

> Churches in the American colonies were debating the relative merits of singing by ear and by note. At the same time, British churches argued about using humans 'of human composure,' particularly by Isaac Watts. One hundred years after Watts died, people would still walk out of a meeting if someone started singing something other than a Psalm set to music.[68]

Churches down through the years have debated how to approach this central element of the worship gathering.

The type of music used in worship has shifted dramatically in recent years. In their fascinating National Congregations Study (NCS) researchers at Duke University discovered,

> Congregations' central activity is corporate worship. This has not changed, but the nature of worship in American congregations has changed noticeably in recent years. One of the most fascinating and important changes is that worship services have become more informal in recent years, with more churches using contemporary music and musical styles, more spontaneous speaking from people in the pews, more unscripted bodily movement, and other developments that make worship more expressive and apparently focused on producing a certain kind of religious experience for participants.[69]

The NCS discovered that from 1998 to 2012 congregations using choirs fell from 54% to 45%, the number of congregations that used drums increased from 20% to 34% and the number of congregations using an organ dropped from 53% to 42%.[70]

Interestingly, while innovative worship music was generally considered a significant factor in the church growth movement, Thom Rainer discovered that the style of music was not a major factor in determining why a previously unchurched person chose to attend a particular church. In fact, in 2001, style of worship or music ranked second-to-last at 11%, followed only by location at 7%.[71]

Preaching in American Churches

A local church's pastor and preaching are consistently noted as the most significant reason people switch congregations. In 2001, Rainer discovered 90% of respondents said the pastor/preaching was a factor when looking for a new church.[72] In 2016, Pew Research Center discovered that 83% of overall respondents, and 94% of Protestant Evangelicals, said that the quality of sermons played an important role in their choice of church.[73] Preaching plays a crucial role in someone's choice of a local church. The form that preaching should take in today's culture is debated.

In his 2007 book, *They Like Jesus But Not the Church*, pastor Dan Kimball asked individuals their feelings about Jesus and local churches.

> Virtually the first thing every single person I talked to said is that they wish church weren't just a sermon but a discussion. They uniformly expressed that they do not want to only sit and listen to a preacher giving a lecture. And it's not because they do not want to learn. They expressed a strong desire to learn the teachings of Jesus and to learn about the Bible. Rather, they feel they can learn better if they can participate and ask questions.[74]

So, should pastors simply forego the traditional lecture-style sermon for a more conversational approach? Haddon Robinson, in his textbook *Biblical Preaching*, sympathized with the tension pastors often feel. He wrote,

> Those in the pulpit face the pressing temptation to deliver some message other than that of Scripture – a political system . . . a theory of economics, a new religious philosophy, old religious slogans, or a trend in psychology.[75]

However, he still argued, "The type of preaching that best carries the force of divine authority is expository preaching."[76]

John MacArthur agrees:

> Expository preaching is the declarative genre in which inerrancy finds its logical expression and the church has its life and power. Stated simply, inerrancy demands exposition as the only method of preaching that preserves the purity of Scripture and accomplishes the purpose for which God gave us His Word.[77]

So, Kimball believes many people prefer a discussion, while Robinson and MacArthur defend expository preaching. What are we as pastors to do? Is there a preaching model that can combine the necessity of expository preaching with the younger generations' desires to have a conversation instead of listen to a lecture?

In their 2019 book, *Groups That Revitalize*, Kenneth Priest and Alan Stoddard argue helpfully for the use of a sermon-based small group model.[78] This approach allows a pastor to keep the priority of expository preaching in place while still allowing for a discussion-based approach in small groups. With this approach, the authority of the Bible is held in high regard through expository sermons given in monologue form while providing a separate context where individuals can interact with the text and the message. With a sermon-based small group approach, the sermon is the focal point during the small group discussion.

Financial Giving in American Churches

In the section on giving in the early church, we looked at Paul's praise of the Macedonian church in 2 Corinthians 8, who gave generously to Paul's ministry, even though they were in poverty. Do American believers follow this pattern of generosity the Macedonian Christians set for us? In 2001, George Barna discovered,

> Believers frequently donate money to their church – but they do not donate very much. Three out of four born-again adults give money to their church in a typical month; almost nine out of ten contribute to their church during the year.[79]

However, he discovered that, of those who gave, the average total donation to churches over the course of a year was just $500. He concluded,

> Most amazing to us was the fact that only 8 percent of all Christians tithed during that year. In fact, twice as many believers (16 percent) gave nothing to their church as gave 10 percent or more of their income.[80]

In a separate study conducted in 2013, the Barna Group reported that 5% of Americans tithed to a charitable or religious organization in 2012, while 12% of born-again Christians (both evangelical and non-evangelical) tithed.[81]

Brad Waggoner also surveyed followers of Christ about their financial giving. He discovered, "Not quite six out of ten churchgoers said they give even if they're not sure they have enough money."[82] Additionally, 27% strongly agreed that they give regardless of their financial situation, while 19% either said they disagreed somewhat or disagreed strongly with the statement.[83]

Based on these numbers, American believers fall far short of the biblical example set by the Macedonian believers.

How Can We Recover a Devotion to Worship?

There is simply no substitute for gathering every week with a body of believers in a local church to worship the Almighty God. Don Whitney explains well:

> There's an element of worship and the Christian life that can never be experienced in private worship or by watching worship. There are some graces and blessings that our Father gives only when we 'meet together' with other believers as His family.[84]

Pastor, like so many other things in the life of a church, worship begins with you. How do you approach the Sunday morning gathering? Do you sing passionately during the musical worship, or is your nose buried in your sermon notes? (I am not condemning you – I have been guilty of that before.) Do you model giving generously to the local church? Do you preach with conviction and passion, or do you just "go through the motions" during your sermon? When you interact with your folks before and after the service, do your words and body language convey that gathering with the local body to worship brings you joy, or does your face tell a different story?

As you evaluate your weekly worship gathering, is your order of service built around entertaining your people or is it built around edifying them, educating them, and leading them to worship the almighty, holy, sovereign Creator of the universe?[85] If you seek to do the latter, over time I suspect you will see an increased engagement from your people in Sunday worship.

As I mentioned previously, I wrote this book in the middle of the COVID-19 crisis in the spring of 2020. During that time, the vast majority of churches suspended in-person worship gatherings for a time in the interest of public health. While I am grateful for the technology that allowed us to continue sharing the gospel virtually and encouraging believers during those days, watching a worship service on a smartphone screen was a terrible substitute for being able to gather in the same room as the body of Christ.

The early believers met weekly to worship together in the first century. As we enter the third decade of the 21st Century, corporate worship is still an essential element for growing disciples.

While recovering a biblical idea of worship goes far beyond music, we saw that music played a key role in the early church's worship. I think it is fascinating that with so much attention given to music styles over the past 30 years, and with so much emphasis on playing the right *kind* of music to get people in the doors, church attendance has steadily declined over that period. Could it be that we spent all this time focusing on the wrong thing, especially since it appears that music does not play a significant role in many peoples' decisions to attend – or to not attend – a particular church?

When it comes to our choice of songs in worship, I think we should have a mix of older and newer songs. As Bill Mounce pointed out above, the early believers in Acts likely sang songs both older songs from Psalms as well as newer songs about the life of Christ. It is even possible that a passage like Philippians 2:5-11 was an early Christian hymn.

If you are a worship leader reading this, do not be afraid of singing older hymns (with or without the optional Chris Tomlin chorus), songs written within the last decade, or anything in between. The Lord values songs that have sound theology from all different time periods and settings and reflecting a variety of styles.

Prayer for the Journey

Father, I thank you for the example of worship that the early believers in Acts set for us. Give me a passion for worshiping you the way they did. When we gather, may we feel the same sense of awe that the first believers felt when they were together. May our worship not just be a routine reserved for Sunday mornings, but may we also offer our lives to you as living sacrifices of praise. Amen.

TAKE ACTION

1. Look back over your church's worship gathering order of service over the past month. Take a look at the songs that were sung. Consider the announcements that were made. Look over your sermon notes. Was the order of service geared more toward entertaining the attendees or worshiping the Almighty God? If the former, what steps can you take to turn your congregations' attention and affections to the Father, the Son and the Holy Spirit during the worship gathering?

2. Does your church tend to lean more toward singing traditional hymns or newer worship songs? Why is that? If your service skews more toward one side, what would happen if you incorporated more of the other in your worship service?

3. Take a look at your own financial giving to your local church over the past six months. Are you modeling what giving generously should look like for your church body? If not, what expenses can you cut in order to give more generously?

4. This coming Sunday, pay attention to your mood as you greet people before and after the service. If you have a security camera system, perhaps you could go back and watch your body language during your interactions with your folks. Are you exuding joy or something else? If you video record your services, go back and watch how you welcomed folks, how you made announcements, and yes, even your sermon. Did you convey a sense of awe and worship? Or were you "just going through the motions?"

Further reading on corporate worship:

- *Worship Essentials* by Mike Harland
- *Spiritual Disciplines for the Christian Life* by Donald S. Whitney
- *Celebration of Discipline* by Richard J. Foster
- *Worship Matters* by Bob Kauflin

Further reading on preaching:

- *Biblical Preaching* by Haddon W. Robinson
- *Preach* by Mark Dever
- *The Shepherd Preacher* by Mark Hallock
- *Preaching by the Book* by R. Scott Pace

Further reading on financial giving:

- *The Money Challenge* by Art Rainer

chapter 6

THEY DEVOTED THEMSELVES...
TO EVANGELISM

Go, therefore, and make disciples of all nations, baptizing them in the name of the Father and of the Son and of the Holy Spirit.
Matthew 28:19

This evangelistic work of declaring the gospel is the primary ministry that the church has toward the world.
Wayne Grudem[86]

Luke concludes his description of the early church in Acts 2:42-47 by saying, "Every day the Lord added to their number those who were being saved." The book of Acts is replete with examples of the apostles and others sharing the gospel with those around them.

Jesus' final command to His disciples to evangelize is recorded in the gospels of Matthew and Luke. In what has become known as the Great Commission, Jesus commanded His disciples to "Go, therefore, and make disciples of all nations, baptizing them in the name of the Father and of the Son and of the Holy Spirit" (Matthew 28:19).

The English word for evangelism comes from the Greek word *evangelizo*, which means "to bring a message, to announce good news."[87] It is used most often to refer to preaching. Mounce explained, "The word is used primarily in the specialized sense of preaching the gospel, that is, God's message of salvation through Jesus Christ."[88]

While the word evangelism is not present in Acts 2:42-47, the concept is clearly present throughout the book. Just before this passage, Luke recorded Peter's powerful evangelistic sermon on the day of Pentecost when 3,000 people came to faith in Christ (Acts 2:41). Throughout Acts, Luke wrote about the incredible explosion in the number of believers throughout the known world (See Appendix B: Kingdom Expansion in Acts for a detailed look at the expansion of the church throughout the book of Acts).

The book of Acts covers roughly 30 years from Jesus' ascension to Paul's imprisonment in Rome. The growth in the number of believers from 120 gathered in a single room in Acts 1:15 to many thousands throughout the known world by the end of the book is staggering.[89] How did the number of believers grow so rapidly? The answer, in the simplest of terms, is evangelism.

Evangelism in the Early Church

In Acts 1:8 Luke recorded a key promise Jesus made to His disciples related to evangelism. "But you will receive power when the Holy Spirit has come on you, and you will be my witnesses in Jerusalem, in all Judea and Samaria, and to the end of the earth." Kent Hughes, writing on this passage, says,

> Verse 8 is the key verse of the entire book of Acts. Chapters 1-7 tell of the witness "in Jerusalem," chapters 8-11 the witness "[in all Judea and Samaria,' and chapters 12-28 the witness 'to the end of the earth."[90]

Jesus' first assignment for the disciples to begin sharing the gospel was right where they already were — Jerusalem. In fact, the first seven chapters of Acts deal exclusively with the activity of the early believers in the city. After Stephen's martyrdom described in Acts 7, Luke writes in Acts 8:1, "all except the apostles were scattered throughout the land of Judea and Samaria." Persecution ultimately drove the believers out of Jerusalem into Judea and Samaria. As they went, they did exactly what Jesus told them they would do. They were witnesses to all they had seen and heard from the apostles. The rest of the book of Acts records the gospel's spread throughout the rest of the known world, culminating with the Apostle Paul living under house arrest in Rome.

There is a common theme in the book of Acts: men and women responded to the gospel; they turned from sin, trusted in Christ and were saved. However, this only happened as men and women were faithful to share the good news of the gospel message to those around them. Believers sharing the good news with the lost around them is the means God has chosen to use to spread the gospel.

While space does not allow me to recount here every evangelistic conversation and conversion in the book of Acts, I want to focus on three such instances: the Ethiopian official in

Acts 8, Cornelius and his household in Acts 10 and the Philippian jailer in Acts 16.

Acts 8: the Ethiopian Official

In Acts 8:26, Luke writes, "An angel of the Lord spoke to Philip: 'Get up and go south to the road that goes down from Jerusalem to Gaza.'" In v. 27, Philip obeyed, and there he met "an Ethiopian man, a eunuch and high official of Candace, queen of the Ethiopians, who was in charge of her entire treasury." The Holy Spirit told Philip to go near the chariot. Verse 30 says, "When Philip ran up to it, he heard him reading the prophet Isaiah, and said, 'Do you understand what you're reading?'" The eunuch responded by asking how he could unless someone guided him. Luke tells us that the passage the eunuch was reading was from Isaiah 53:7-8. Then Luke explained, "Philip proceeded to tell him the good news about Jesus, beginning with that Scripture."

Luke wrote that they then came to some water and

> The eunuch said, "Look, there's water. What would keep me from being baptized?" So he ordered the chariot to stop and both Philip and the eunuch went down into the water, and he baptized him.

Acts 10: Cornelius and His Family

In Acts 10, Luke recorded the story of Cornelius. In v. 1, he writes that Cornelius was "a centurion of what was called the Italian Regiment." Luke further explains in v. 2, "He was a devout man and feared God along with his whole household. He did many charitable deeds for the Jewish people and always prayed to God." In verse 5, Cornelius dreamed of an angel who came to him, saying, "Send men to Joppa and call for Simon, who is also named Peter. He is lodging with Simon, a tanner whose house is by the sea." After the dream ended, Cornelius sent his men to find Peter in v. 8.

As they were traveling, Luke wrote that Peter went up to the roof to pray. He became hungry and wanted something to eat. While his food was prepared, he fell into a trance. He saw heaven opened and an object like a large sheet coming down, being lowered by its four corners to the earth. In it were all the four-footed animals and reptiles of the earth and the birds of the sky. A voice said to him in v. 13, "Get up, Peter; kill and eat."

Peter protested, saying he had never eaten anything unclean. The voice responded in v. 15 by saying, "What God has made clean, do not call impure." Luke says this occurred three times, in v. 16, "suddenly the object was taken up into heaven." As Peter considered what the dream might mean, in v. 17, the men Cornelius sent arrived.

After Cornelius' men explained the purpose of their visit, Peter went with them back to Cornelius. When he arrived, he explained to Cornelius that it was forbidden for a Jew to associate with a foreigner. But, through the vision, God revealed that he should not call anything clean that God has made clean. Peter then preached the good news of Christ to Cornelius and his household. In v. 47, Peter asked, "Can anyone withhold water and prevent these people from being baptized, who have received the Holy Spirit just as we have?" In v. 48, Peter commanded them to be baptized in the name of Jesus Christ.

This passage is significant because not only does it show the radical salvation of nonbelievers, but it also shows the gospel going to Gentiles. This message of the gospel was no longer for Jews only: it is for the whole world!

Acts 16: the Philippian Jailer

In Acts 16, Paul and Silas were arrested after casting a demon out of a slave girl. In 16:17, Luke explained that this girl followed Paul for many days, crying out, "These men, who are proclaiming to you the way of salvation, are the servants of the Most High God." Finally, Paul, greatly annoyed, turned around and cast the demon out. According to Luke, the girl made her owners a large profit by fortune-telling. Verse 19 says, "When her owners realized that their hope of profit was gone, they seized Paul and Silas and dragged them off into the marketplace to the authorities."

That evening, Paul and Silas were in prison. Luke records in 16:25, "About midnight Paul and Silas were praying and singing hymns to God, and the prisoners were listening to them." Suddenly a violent earthquake shook the foundations of the jail, all the doors flew open and the shackles fell off the prisoners. As the jailer woke up and realized that the doors of the prison were open, he prepared to kill himself. Paul then called out in a loud voice in v. 28, "Do not harm yourself, because we're all here!"

The jailer rushed in and fell down before Paul, asking him, "What must I do to be saved?" What, exactly, did the jailer mean by this? I think he was literally scared for his life! If his prisoners escaped, his physical life could be on the line, hence the reason he was about to commit suicide. But Paul uses this man's question to point him to his greatest need: spiritual life and relationship with God.

Paul told the jailer he needed to believe in the Lord Jesus Christ to be saved from sin and death, he and his household. The jailer responded to the gospel message from Paul and Silas with faith, and in v. 34, "he brought them into his house, set a meal before them, and rejoiced because he had come to believe in God with his entire household."

Sharing and Believing the Good News

These three stories from Acts illustrate three very different individuals — an Ethiopian eunuch, a Roman centurion and a Philippian jailer — who came to faith in Christ through the same means: the evangelistic efforts of early disciples. We see the powerful effect of the gospel upon the lives of these three men. We also see examples of two apostles and one layman faithfully sharing the gospel and God keeping His promise to save people — even entire families — through the message of Jesus' life, death and resurrection!

Evangelism in American Churches

Believers in the early church faithfully shared the gospel, obeying Jesus' command in Matthew 28, and as they did, the kingdom of God expanded rapidly throughout the world. How are followers of Christ in the United States in the 21st century doing with carrying out Jesus' mandate? Not very well.

In 2007, Brad Waggoner asked 2,500 respondents, "Is it every Christian's responsibility to share the gospel with non-Christians?" He discovered that 46% said they "agreed strongly" while another 26% said they "agreed somewhat," for a total positive response of 72%.[91] When asked if they felt comfortable sharing their belief in Christ with someone else effectively, only 28% said they "strongly agreed," while another 48% said they "agreed somewhat."[92] So, 72% of respondents agreed that they were called to share their faith, and 76% said they at least somewhat agreed that they would be comfortable sharing their faith. It may seem that a three-quarters majority in these areas is not bad, however, I think it should concern us that only 46% of respondents said they believed they had a responsibility to share the gospel with non-Christians, and only 26% felt confident in sharing their faith.

Things took a further downward turn when Waggoner asked respondents how much they agreed or disagreed with the statement, "I intentionally spend time building friendships with non-Christians for the purpose of sharing Christ with them."[93] Only seven percent said they "strongly agreed" and another 18% "agreed somewhat" with the statement. So, while 72% of respondents agreed that evangelism is every believer's responsibility, only 25% said they actively built relationships with non-Christians for the purpose of sharing the gospel with them. Waggoner's survey then asked respondents how many times they had personally shared the gospel with someone in the past six months. "Twenty-nine percent of our sample said they had shared Christ at least twice in the prior six months, 14 percent had done that once, and 57 percent said, 'not at all.'"[94] This means more than half of the respondents in Waggoner's study in 2007 said they had not shared their faith in Christ with someone else in the past six months.

In 2013, the Barna Group also conducted a study regarding the evangelistic habits of born-again Christians. They discovered:

> When asked if they have a personal responsibility to share their faith with others, 73% of born again [sic] Christians said yes. When this conviction is put into practice, however, the numbers shift downward. Only half (52%) of born again [sic] Christians say they actually did share the Gospel at least once this past year to someone with different beliefs, in the hope that they might accept Jesus Christ as their Savior.[95]

In this Barna study, the numbers are more encouraging when we look at those who identify as Evangelicals. Barna discovered that 100% of Evangelicals affirmed the belief that they are supposed to share their faith with others, while nearly 70% said they had done so in the last year.[96] While these results are more encouraging than those from the Waggoner study, I do not know a single pastor who would be content with his church receiving a C grade (and barely that) when it comes to evangelism.

When we look at these statistics, Mark Dever's words certainly ring true:

> "Flunk" is a word we do not use much anymore. It is a hard, sharp, inflexible kind of word. But it is probably a good word to use to quickly summarize how most of us have done in obeying the call to evangelize.[97]

Don Whitney notes, ironically, how the gospel arrived in America in the first place:

> For the command of Jesus to be fulfilled and for Americans to hear about Christ, the gospel had to come here by other Christians who understood that they, too, were charged with going to "all nations."[98]

The verdict is clear: American Christians are not effectively sharing the gospel with a lost and dying world.

How Can We Recover a Devotion to Evangelism?

I want to focus on two motivations for evangelism. First, we should be motivated to evangelize by our love for and obedience to the Savior. Scripture makes it clear that Jesus expected His followers to tell others the good news of the gospel (Matt. 28:18-20; Acts 1:8). If followers of Christ want to be obedient to God's call on their lives, they must evangelize. Whitney says, "Godliness requires that we discipline ourselves in the practice of evangelism."[99] This is far from a cold obedience, but one that is driven out of 1) a deep love for Christ and 2) an understanding of what Christ has done for us by rescuing us from spiritual death and giving us new life (Eph. 2:1-5, 2 Cor. 5:17).

Our goal in evangelism cannot be to "close the sale," as it were, but to be faithful to Christ's command to share the gospel. Michael Lawrence helpfully explains:

> The biblical doctrine of evangelism has enormous implications for our approach to evangelism. If conversion is the result of God's work of giving us new hearts that repent and believe the gospel, then evangelism is not a sales method. It's not about identifying felt needs and shaping the gospel product accordingly . . . Evangelism is faithfully communicating an authoritative message from God, one that warns us about our very real need, whether we feel it or not. It's that message that requires a very particular response. And it is that message that, remarkably, converts sinners like you and me by the power of the Holy Spirit.[100]

When our motivation for sharing the gospel is a love for Christ and appreciation for what He has done to save us, we will avoid tactics aimed at generating a decision for Christ divorced from a commitment to follow Him. When Christ's love compels us to share the gospel, we will share out of a desire to see others taste the goodness of the gospel that we have experienced and respond with genuine repentance and faith.

The second motivation is love for people around us. Each of us has neighbors, coworkers, family and friends who do not know Christ Jesus as Savior and Lord. We are surrounded by people whom the Bible tells us are separated from Almighty God because of their sin. If we genuinely believe that, then the most loving thing we can do is share the best news we know: the good news of Jesus! This good news centers on the promise of new life in Christ; of hearts that were dead in sin awakening to life in relationship with God.

One practical way that we show our love for our neighbors (Matt. 22:39) is by sharing the truth of the gospel with them. Some people will see our attempts at evangelism as merely a condemnation of an ungodly lifestyle. We need to honestly evaluate this critique. If our evangelistic message is merely that we think people need to change their bad habits and clean up their lives then we are communicating a false gospel. The problem goes much deeper than people needing to cease bad habits; they actually need to repent of sinful rebellion against the Creator of the universe! They need to turn from a life of sin and death to a life alive in Christ. Our message cannot be: bad people become good. It must be dead people receive life. That is the promise of the gospel.

Sharing the Good News

How do we go about sharing the gospel with those around us? Well, you start sharing. There is no magic formula. The incredible thing about the gospel is that, no matter how much the culture around us may change, the old, old story never changes. We proclaim the same gospel that Paul declared in 1 Corinthians 15.

One way to evangelize is to simply share Paul's words in 1 Corinthians 15:3-4: "For I passed on to you as most important what I also received: that Christ died for our sins according to the Scriptures, that he was buried, that he was raised on the third day according to the Scriptures."

Bob Burton, sending church coach and pipeline specialist for the North American Mission Board writes,

> Despite the incredible technological advancements in the world, the twenty-first century church has the same Holy Spirit, the same Word of God, the same gospel message, and the same opportunities the early church did.[101]

With all the changes we see happening so rapidly in our culture, may we never lose sight of the fact that the same gospel message that has saved countless millions over the past 2,000 years still has the power to save today.

Actions that Match our Message

There's a short but important phrase in Acts 2:47 that, I believe, had a large impact on the effectiveness of the early church's evangelism efforts. The first half of v. 47 says that the believers were "praising God and enjoying the favor of all the people." They enjoyed the favor of the people. In that phrase, Luke tells us that believers had a good reputation in their community, that they had formed good relationships.

How did they cultivate those relationships? I think, in many ways, that reputation was a culmination of everything we have seen so far in this book. They had a good relationship because they were devoted to Scripture not only in words but also in the way they lived. They were people who enjoyed the fellowship of other believers. They understood they had a deep bond with those in the body of Christ. They sacrificed by selling their possessions and property to meet needs within the church. They were people of prayer – when they said they were going to pray for someone, they actually did it (maybe even right there on the spot in the market or in their living room). They were a worshipful people – when they spoke of their adoration for the Lord, it matched their lifestyle. The believers in the early church built relationships that opened the door to sharing the gospel by devoting themselves to the Word, to fellowship and the breaking of bread, to prayer ... in sum by devoting themselves to Christ through a life of worship.

When I think of someone who models a lifestyle of evangelism, I immediately think of my friend Matt Queen. Queen is the Scarborough Chair of Evangelism at the Southwestern Baptist Theological Seminary, and he is also one of the most faithful personal evangelists I have ever encountered. He is not just a professor of evangelism; he is a practitioner of it. I have never been to a restaurant with him when he did not share the gospel with our waiter or waitress. He constantly turns conversations to the person of Jesus, and he does so in a natural way. He often simply asks, as the food is being served, "Has anyone told you today that Jesus loves you?"

I am amazed at how many people stop cold in their tracks at that question (especially in the foodservice industry, where waiters and waitresses hear far more about how customers are unhappy than they hear that Someone truly loves them). And I have yet to see any server refuse when Matt asks how he can pray for them before we eat.

Queen's example reminds me of my own shortfalls in evangelism, but it also makes me want to share Jesus with the same passion and enthusiasm that he does.[102] Maybe he sums it up best when he says, "Anyone who knows enough of the Gospel to have heard it, believed it, and been saved by it, knows enough of the Gospel to share it."[103] If you or your church are feeling a bit stagnate in your evangelism efforts, I highly recommend Queen's book *Mobilize to Evangelize*. It is a simple workbook that will lead you as a pastor to evaluate your church's evangelism and take practical steps to become more intentional about sharing the gospel.

We cannot divorce the reputation of our churches (and church members) from our evangelistic efforts. If we are seen as hypocrites in our communities, as people who do not live out what we say we believe, that will hamper the evangelistic reach we have. However, if we are seen as people who genuinely live out what we say we believe – however imperfectly we may do so – it will open the door to evangelistic conversations with people all around us.

So, how well does your church show that you actually believe what you say you believe about the gospel? And what changes do you need to make so that your actions match your message?

Prayer for the Journey

Father, I repent of my failure to tell those close to me about the hope that is found only in the gospel. Give me boldness to faithfully proclaim the message of Christ's life, death and resurrection. I pray that as people hear the message, you would change their hearts and lead them to turn from sin to faith in Christ. Thank you for the blessing of knowing You, and the privilege of proclaiming the gospel to those around me. Amen.

TAKE ACTION

— · — · — · — · —

1. Think back to the last conversation you had about the gospel with someone who does not know Jesus as Savior. Who was it with? How did it go? Were you nervous?

2. In a typical week, how many gospel conversations do you think your members are having in their schools, neighborhoods, workplaces and homes? Are you encouraged or discouraged by that number? How can you train and/or encourage your members to more regularly share their faith?

3. If you were asked to explain the gospel in three sentences or less, what would you say? Write your response below.

Further reading on evangelism:

- *Mobilize to Evangelize: The Pastor and Effective Congregational Evangelism* by Matt Queen

- *The Gospel and Personal Evangelism* by Mark Dever

- *The Master Plan of Evangelism* by Robert E. Coleman

- *The Spiritual DNA of a Church on Mission* by Bob Burton

chapter 7

BECOMING A 1ˢᵗ CENTURY CHURCH
IN THE 21ˢᵗ CENTURY

Now to Him who is able to do above and beyond all that we ask
or think according to the power that works in us - to Him be
glory in the church and in Christ Jesus to all generations,
forever and ever. Amen.
Ephesians 3:20-21

God clearly has decided to use the church - and only the
church - as the means by which his gospel will go to the ends
of the earth.
David Platt[104]

Throughout this book, we have focused on a short passage of
Scripture at the end of one of the most powerful chapters in the
entire New Testament. Here it is again:

> They devoted themselves to the apostles' teaching, to the
> fellowship, to the breaking of bread, and to prayer. Everyone was
> filled with awe, and many wonders and signs were being

performed through the apostles. Now all the believers were together and held all things in common. They sold their possessions and property and distributed the proceeds to all, as any had need. Every day they devoted themselves to meeting together in the temple, and broke bread from house to house. They ate their food with joyful and sincere hearts, praising God and enjoying the favor of all the people. Every day the Lord added to their number those who were being saved," (Acts 2:42-47).

Let's take a minute to consider all the disciples had experienced in the weeks leading up to this passage.

At the end of the Passover festival, the disciples witnessed Jesus' enemies arrest Him, beat Him and crucify Him. Or at least, they were aware that these things were going on. In reality, all of the 12 disciples except for John ran away. They abandoned Jesus in the greatest time of distress He experienced on earth. Peter denied that he even knew Jesus three times. Judas handed Jesus over to be crucified. John is the only disciple we are told was at the cross.

Imagine what they experienced that Friday night and Saturday. We have no record of what happened on that Saturday. I am curious how the disciples responded as they tried to wrap their minds around everything that just happened. Then, to top it all off, some of the other believers came to them early on Sunday morning saying that Jesus' body had disappeared.

A short time later, the resurrected Lord appeared to them. Suddenly they remembered all He taught them during His ministry. Jesus spent 40 more days teaching them until He was taken up to heaven before their very eyes. After this, the disciples just kind of stood around looking into the sky, when two angels finally speak to them in Acts 1:11, saying, "Men of

Galilee, why do you stand looking up into heaven? This same Jesus, who has been taken from you into heaven, will come in the same way that you have seen him going into heaven." In other words, the angels ask, "Hey guys, what are you waiting for? Jesus told you what to do ... so go do it!" And they do.

These men share the gospel. Ten days later, on the day of Pentecost, the Holy Spirit falls on all the believers, as they are gathered for worship. On that day, Peter preaches the gospel and 3,000 people are saved. The church in Jerusalem grew from around 120 in chapter one, to more than 3,000 in chapter two, to many thousands of believers around the known world by the end of the book.

Fast forward nearly 2,000 years, and many people are sounding dire warnings about the state of Christianity. Some of the warnings are needed. For instance, between 2017 and 2018, the denomination I am a part of, the Southern Baptist Convention, saw its number of churches by more than 1,100. Some left because of theological differences, but at least half of them closed their doors. Many in our culture are ready to declare the end of Christianity's influence in America.

Devotion to Christ

As pastors in these days, we must consider and take to heart the words of Acts 2:42-47. The principles in this passage do not depend upon smoke machines, spotlights or HD projectors. They do not rely on multi-million-dollar sanctuaries with comfortable chairs and thermostats always set at 71.5 degrees.

As the church in Jerusalem devoted themselves to Christ by devoting themselves to Scripture, fellowship, prayer, worship and evangelism, God did a mighty work in and through His people. The gospel advanced powerfully, even in days of intense persecution.

Maybe you look at the people in your church and wonder, "Is there any way God could use these folks like he used the folks in Acts?" That's an excellent question. Let's end this journey together by looking at the people God used in Acts.

The People Who Turned the World Upside Down

In many ways, I am envious of the men and women who were a part of the first church because of what they got to experience. Many of them experienced the ministry of Jesus first-hand. Ten days after they watched Jesus ascend into heaven, Acts 2:3-4 tells us the first believers were all together in one place when suddenly, something extraordinary happened:

> They saw tongues like flames of fire that separated and rested on each one of them. Then they were all filled with the Holy Spirit and began to speak in different tongues, as the Spirit enabled them.

Now, let's be honest. If flaming tongues were suddenly flying toward me, I would probably pass out on the spot. That just doesn't happen. And yet, this is how God the Father chose to impart the Holy Spirit to the first believers.

In verse 4, Luke tells us that all the people began to speak in other tongues. In this context, Luke is talking about real languages. So, all the believers are gathered together when suddenly flaming tongues come on each person. The next thing they know, they are all speaking in different languages.

This becomes even more amazing when verse 5 tells us that there were people from "every nation under heaven" living in Jerusalem. People from all over the known world were in Jerusalem, and suddenly they hear people speaking in their native tongue. What happens here in Acts 2, is the reversal of what happened at Babel in Genesis 11. There we see the confusion that resulted when people worshipped themselves. In Acts 2, all the believers were together praising God, and an incredible moment of worship happens. Instead of making their own names great, which the people attempted at Babel, these men and women end up taking the Gospel throughout the known world. They made God's name great. Babel was about the love of self; Acts 2 is about the love of the Savior.

As you might imagine, there was quite a bit of confusion after these events in Acts 2. Those who witnessed everything that just happened were not quite sure what to make of it. In Acts 2:12-13, we read, "They were all astounded and perplexed, saying to one another, 'What does this mean?' But some sneered and said, 'They're drunk on new wine.'"

Think about those two reactions: some were amazed, while others mocked. Here we are, almost 2,000 years later, and people respond to the gospel the same way people did at Pentecost. Some are amazed and lay down their lives before the throne of God. Others mock. Our responsibility today is to share the gospel as those early believers did and trust God with the response we get.

In Acts 2, Peter did just that. Hearing those in the watching crowd mocking, Peter stands up and boldly proclaims the gospel. I love that Peter is entrusted with the leadership of the early church. Why? Because when I look at Peter, I realize that he did not have it all together. When I see the way Peter responded to situations, I see reflections of myself.

Sometimes he knocked it out of the park, like in Matthew 16:15-17. In that passage, Jesus asks His disciples what others are saying about Him. The disciples respond by saying, "Some say Moses, some say Elijah or one of the other prophets." Then Jesus makes it personal by asking them, "Who do you say that I am?" Peter does not skip a beat:

> You are the Messiah, the Son of the living God," He says. Jesus praises Peter for his answer, "Blessed are you, Simon, son of Jonah, because flesh and blood did not reveal this to you, but my Father in heaven.

I imagine the other disciples high-fiving Peter. "Way to go, Peter! You rock!" But, then, just a few verses later, Peter completely blows it.

Jesus followed up Peter's confession in Matthew 16 by telling His disciples what was about to happen to Him in Jerusalem. He explained that He would suffer at the hands of the elders, chief priests and scribes in Jerusalem. He tells them that He will be killed, but then raised on the third day. At this point, Peter -- the same Peter who made such an astonishing confession just a couple of paragraphs before -- pipes up and says, "Oh no, Lord! This will never happen to you."

This time Jesus has an altogether different response for him: "Get behind me, Satan. You are a hindrance to me because you're not thinking about God's concerns but human concerns." I am no genius, but I am thinking that having Jesus call him Satan was probably not a high point in the life of Peter. Look at the difference in just a few verses! Sometimes Peter had the right answer, and at other times he was clueless.

I see a lot of myself in Peter. At times I say exactly what I think should be said in a situation and the next minute I'm trying to pull my foot out of my mouth – and its way in there! In Scripture, God does not cover over the flaws of the characters. Noah got drunk and fell asleep naked. Abraham feared Pharaoh more than God. Joseph was a spoiled brat. Moses was a stutterer with low self-esteem. David was an adulterer. Jonah's preaching led to one of the greatest revivals in history, and he was livid about it. Paul was a murderer of Christians. And God used all of them in mighty ways.

In Acts 2, Peter, this fisherman with an overactive temper, preaches the gospel. And what happens? Men, women and children are saved. And here we are, 2,000 years later on the other side of the world, and the gospel is still being proclaimed and people are still being saved.

Jesus called guys like Peter and John, fishermen, to follow him. Do you remember the response of the religious leaders when they saw Peter and John preaching? Acts 4:13 says the religious leaders saw their boldness, realized they were uneducated and untrained, and "they were amazed and realized they had been with Jesus."

Wow. What a sentence. The impressive thing about the disciples was not their scholarly intellect or amazing rhetoric: it was that they had been with Jesus. When a lot of pastors and church leaders look at their folks, I wonder how often we see people who are uneducated and untrained? Do not get me wrong, I am a big fan of education and training. But more church members with seminary degrees is not what will change the world. The thing that God uses to change the world is work through people who have spent time with the Master.

In Acts 17, we see an amazing statement about a group of believers who were arrested. They were not arrested because they were smart. They were arrested because it was said, "These men who have turned the world upside down have come here too."[105] That is quite a reputation for a ragtag group of folks who were uneducated and untrained. This should tell us that God can do mighty things through ordinary people who are surrendered to His plans.

May we who are pastors and church leaders plead with the Lord to move again like He did in Acts. And may we devote ourselves to the same things to which the first disciples were devoted. Could it be that the answer to a decline in Christianity is not a new idea, but an ancient one?

And so, this is where we end. Or maybe it is where we begin.

> Paul stayed two whole years in his own rented house. And he welcomed all who visited him, proclaiming the kingdom of God and teaching about the Lord Jesus Christ **with all boldness and without hindrance.** (Acts 28:30-31)

SELECTED PRAYERS IN ACTS

PASSAGE	PEOPLE	TYPE OF PRAYER
Acts 1:14	The church in Jerusalem	Corporate
Acts 2:42	The church in Jerusalem	Corporate and Private
Acts 4:23-31	Peter, John, "their own people" (CSB)	Corporate
Acts 10:9	Peter	Private
Acts 12:5, 12	The church in Jerusalem	Corporate
Acts 13:3	The church in Antioch	Corporate
Acts 16:25	Paul and Silas	Private (with others nearby)

KINGDOM EXPANSION IN ACTS

PASSAGE	DESCRIPTION
Acts 1:15	"About a hundred and twenty."
Acts 2:41	"Three thousand people were added to them."
Acts 2:47	"Every day the Lord added to their number those who were being saved."
Acts 4:4	"The number of the men came to about five thousand."
Acts 5:14	"Believers were added to the Lord in increasing numbers — multitudes of both men and women."
Acts 6:7	"The disciples in Jerusalem increased greatly in number."
Acts 8:1	"All except the apostles were scattered through Judea and Samaria."
Acts 8:4	"Those who were scattered went on their way preaching the Word."
Acts 21:20	"You see, brother, how many thousands of Jews there are who have believed."

NOTES

1 Dietrich Bonhoeffer, *The Cost of Discipleship* (New York: Touchstone, 1995), 89.

2 John Calvin, *Institutes of the Christian Religion,* https://www.ccel.org/ccel/calvin/institutes.iii.xii.html, para. 8).

3 Donald Whitney, *Spiritual Disciplines for the Christian Life* (Colorado Springs, CO: NavPress, 1991, 2014), 22.

4 This is an over-simplified explanation of the process of canonization. For a more in-depth explanation, check out Craig Blomberg's excellent article here: https://www.namb.net/apologetics-blog/the-new-testament-canon.

5 John R. Stott, *The Message of Acts* (Downers Grove, IL: InterVarsity Press, 1990), 82.

6 "The Baptist Faith and Message," http://www.sbc.net/bfm2000/bfm2000.asp.

7 "The Chicago Statement on Biblical Inerrancy," https://www.moodybible.org/beliefs/the-chicago-statement-on-biblical-inerrancy.

8 Brad Waggoner, *The Shape of Faith to Come: Spiritual Formation and the Future of Discipleship* (Nashville, TN: B&H Publishing Group, 2008), 33.

9 Waggoner, 69.

10 A.W. Geiger, "5 Facts on How Americans View the Bible and Other Religious Texts" (2017). Retrieved from http://www.pewresearch.org/fact-tank/2017/04/14/5-facts-on-how-americans-view-the-bible-and-other-religious-texts.

11 Geiger.

12 Whitney, 22.

13 Whitney, 22.

[14] For more on the philosophy behind expositional preaching, I recommend the books *Preach* by Mark Dever and Greg Gilbert, *The Shepherd Preacher* by Mark Hallock and *Preaching by the Book* by R Scott Pace.

[15] Rick Warren, *The Purpose Driven Church: Growth Without Compromising Your Message* (Grand Rapids, MI: Zondervan, 1995), 310.

[16] William Mounce, *William D. Mounce's Complete Expository Dictionary of Old and New Testament Words* (Grand Rapids, MI: Zondervan, 2006), 247.

[17] I.H. Marshall, *Tyndale New Testament Commentary: Acts* (Downers Grove, IL: IVP Academic, 1980), 85.

[18] R. Kent Hughes, *Acts: The Church Afire* (Wheaton, IL: Crossway, 2014), chap. 5, Kindle.

[19] Stott, 83.

[20] Hughes, chap. 9, Kindle.

[21] Isaiah 42:8.

[22] Mark Dever, *Nine Marks of a Healthy Church* (Wheaton, IL: Crossway, 2004), 155.

[23] Dever, 155.

[24] Aaron Earls, "Most Teenagers Drop Out of Church as Young Adults," LifeWay Research, Jan. 15, 2019, https://lifewayresearch.com/2019/01/15/most-teenagers-drop-out-of-church-as-young-adults.

[25] Ibid.

[26] Waggoner, 236.

[27] Charles Colson and Ellen Vaughn, *Being the Body: A New call for the Church to be Light in the Darkness* (Nashville, TN: W Publishing Group, 2003), 107.

[28] Waggoner, 236.

[29] Andy Stanley and Bill Willits, *Creating Community: Five Keys to Building a Small Group Culture* (Colorado Springs, CO: Multnomah Books, 2004), 22.

[30] Stanley and Willits, 24.

[31] Reeder, *Harry L., Embers to a Flame: How God Can Revitalize Your Church* (Philipsburg, NJ: P&R Publishing Company, 2004), 178.

[32] Ibid, 178.

[33] Ibid, 178-179.

[34] Dietrich Bonhoeffer, *Life Together & Prayerbook of the Bible* (Minneapolis, MN: Fortress Press, 2005), 636, Kindle.

[35] Ibid, 649, Kindle.

[36] Warren, 310.

[37] Kenneth Boa, *Conformed to His Image: Biblical and Practical Approaches to Spiritual Formation* (Grand Rapids, MI: Zondervan, 2001), 424.

[38] Roger Steer, *George Müller: Delighted in God* (Geanies House, Fearn, Tain, Ross–shire, Scotland, UK: Christian Focus Publications, LTD, 2008), 193.

[39] There are any number of works that have been written on Muller's life. I would recommend Roger Steer's biography (referenced above) and *The Autobiography of George Muller*.

[40] Hughes, 749-750, Kindle.

[41] Steve Gaines, *Pray Like It Matters: Intimacy and Power Through Prayer* (Tigerville, SC: Auxano Press, 2013), 21.

[42] Bonhoeffer, 155.

[43] Gaines, 13.

[44] Stott, 85.

[45] For a more detailed look at both corporate and private prayers in Acts, reference the table "Selected Prayers in the Book of Acts" in Appendix 1.

[46] George Barna, *Growing True Disciples: New Strategies for Producing Genuine Followers of Christ* (Colorado Springs, CO: Waterbrook Press, 2001), 60.

[47] Waggoner, 54.

[48] "America's Changing Religious Landscape," Pew Research Center, May 12, 2015, http://www.pewforum.org/wp-content/uploads/sites/7/2015/05/RLS-08-26-full-report.pdf.

[49] Boa, 83.

[50] Mike Harland, *Worship Essentials: Growing a Healthy Worship Ministry Without Starting a War!* (Nashville, TN: B&H Publishing Group, 2018), 8-9.

[51] John Calvin, *Institutes of the Christian Religion* (Calvin Translation Society, 2013). iii.xii. Retrieved from https://app.wordsearchbible.lifeway.com.

[52] Whitney, 103-104.

[53] Stott, 85.

[54] Mounce, 810.

[55] W.E. Vine, *An Expository Dictionary of New Testament* Words (Old Tappan, NJ: Fleming H. Revell Company, 1966), 198.

[56] Bob Kauflin, *Worship Matters: Leading Others to Encounter the Greatness of God*, (Wheaton, IL: Crossway, 2008), 98.

[57] Mounce, 548.

[58] S.J. Lawson, "The Priority of Biblical Preaching: An Expository Study of Acts 2:42-47," *Bibliotheca Sacra*, vol. 158 (April-June 2001): 203.

[59] John MacArthur, *The MacArthur Bible Commentary* (Nashville, TN: Thomas Nelson, Inc, 2005), 1610.

[60] Waggoner, 258.

[61] Waggoner, 258.

[62] "America's Changing Religious Landscape," Pew Research Center, May 12, 2015, http://www.pewforum.org/wp-content/uploads/sites/7/2015/05/RLS-08-26-full-report.pdf

[63] Ibid.

[64] Barna, *Growing True Disciples*, 60.

[65] "In U.S. Decline of Christianity Continues at Rapid Pace," Pew Research Center, Oct. 17, 2019, https://www.pewforum.org/2019/10/17/in-u-s-decline-of-christianity-continues-at-rapid-pace/

[66] Ibid, paragraph 8.

[67] Kauflin, 97.

[68] Ibid, 98.

[69] M. Chavez and A. Eagle, "National Congregations Study: The Religious Congregations in 21st Century America," (2015), 9. Retrieved from http://www.soc.duke.edu/natcong/Docs/NCSIII_report_final.pdf.

[70] Ibid.

[71] Thom Rainer, *Surprising Insights from the Unchurched and Proven Ways to Reach Them* (Grand Rapids, MI: Zondervan, 2001), 21.

[72] Ibid.

[73] Pew, "Choosing a New Church or House of Worship" (2016), 15.

[74] Dan Kimball, *They Like Jesus But Not the Church: Insights from Emerging Generations* (Grand Rapids, MI: Baker Books, 2007), 218.

[75] Haddon W. Robinson, *Biblical Preaching: The Development and Delivery of Expository Messages* (Grand Rapids, MI: Baker Academic, 2014), 3-4.

[76] Ibid, 4.

[77] John MacArthur, *Preaching: How to Preach Biblically* (Nashville, TN: Thomas Nelson, Inc, 2005), 18-19.

[78] Kenneth Priest and Alan Stoddard, *Groups that Revitalize: Bringing New Life to Your Church through Sermon-Based Small Groups* (Littleton, CO: Acoma Press, 2019).

[79] Barna, *Growing True Disciples* (2001), 73-74.

[80] Barna, *Growing True Disciples* (2001), 74.

[81] Barna Group, "American Donor Trends," June 2, 2013, paragraph 12, https://www.barna.com/research/american-donor-trends.

[82] Waggoner, 198.

[83] Ibid.

[84] Whitney, 111.

[85] For more on each of these models and the shortfalls of each, see Reeder, 168-172.

[86] Wayne Grudem, *Systematic Theology: An Introduction to Biblical Doctrine* (Grand Rapids, MI: Zondervan, 1994), 867-868.

[87] Mounce, 220.

[88] Ibid, 533.

[89] For a more complete picture of the exponential growth of believers throughout the book, see Appendix B, "Kingdom Expansion in Acts."

[90] Hughes (2014), chap. 1, Kindle.

[91] Waggoner, 153.

[92] Ibid, 159.

[93] Ibid, 164.

[94] Ibid, 170.

[95] Barna Group, "Is Evangelism Going Out of Style?" December 17, 2013, paragraph 2, https://www.barna.com/research/is-evangelism-going-out-of-style.

[96] Ibid, paragraph 4.

[97] Mark Dever, *The Gospel and Personal Evangelism* (Wheaton, IL: Crossway, 2007), 19.

[98] Whitney, 121.

[99] Ibid, 119.

[100] Michael Lawrence, *Conversion: How God Creates a People* (Wheaton, IL: Crossway, 2017), 90-91.

[101] Bob Burton, *The Spiritual DNA of a Church on Mission: Rediscovering the 1st Century Church for 21st Century Spiritual Awakening* (Nashville, TN: Wordsearch Academic, 2020), 96.

[102] As a side note, Matt also enjoys leading large groups of people in singing Happy Birthday to folks (i.e., me) when it is not, in fact, their (my) birthday. This happened twice. Neither instance involved cake.

[103] Matt Queen, *Mobilize to Evangelize: The Pastor and Effective Congregational Evangelism* (Fort Worth, TX: Seminary Hill Press, 2018), 87.

[104] David Platt, *Radical: Taking Back Your Faith from the American Dream* (Colorado Springs, CO: Multnomah Books, 2010), 157.

[105] Acts 17:6.

Made in the USA
Monee, IL
07 November 2020